How to Get Rid of a Narcissist

7 Proven Strategies to Identify, Confront, and Free Yourself from Narcissistic Influence and Reclaim Your Health and Emotional Well-being.

WHITNEY BARTON

© **Copyright 2024 - All rights reserved.**

The content inside this book may not be duplicated, reproduced, or transmitted without direct written permission from the author or publisher.

Under no circumstances will any blame or legal responsibility be held against the publisher, or author, for any damages, reparation, or monetary loss due to the information contained within this book, either directly or indirectly.

Legal Notice:

This book is copyright protected. It is only for personal use. You cannot amend, distribute, sell, use, quote or paraphrase any part, or the content within this book, without the consent of the author or publisher.

Disclaimer Notice:

Please note the information contained within this document is for educational and entertainment purposes only. All effort has been executed to present accurate, reliable, up to date, complete information. No warranties of any kind are declared or implied. Readers acknowledge that the author is not engaging in the rendering of legal, financial, medical, or professional advice. The content within this book has been derived from various sources. Please consult a licensed professional before attempting any techniques outlined in this book.

By reading this document, the reader agrees that under no circumstances is the author responsible for any losses, direct or indirect, that are incurred as a result of the use of the information contained within this document, including, but not limited to, errors, omissions, or inaccuracies.

TABLE OF CONTENT

INTRODUCTION   5
PART 1: Understanding The Narcissist   7
CHAPTER ONE: Unmasking the Narc: Recognize the Signs and Traits   9

Two Faces of the Narcissist: Grandiose and Vulnerable Narcissistic Types   13
Love Bombing and Devaluing: Deciphering the Narcissistic Cycle of Abuse   18
Gaslighting and Projection: Unmasking the Narcissist's Favorite Manipulation Tactics   22

CHAPTER TWO: Narcissistic Victim Syndrome: The Impact Of Narcissistic Abuse   27

Emotional and Mental Impact: Recognize the Signs of Anxiety, Depression, and PTSD   30
Physical Impact: The Toll of Narcissistic Abuse on Your Body   33
Shattered Self-Esteem and Self-Worth: How the Narcissist Assaults Your Sense of Self   36

CHAPTER THREE: Breaking Free From The Web: Why You Need To Leave   40

Stages of Change: What It Takes to Leave a Narcissist   41
Facing the Fear of Abandonment: Build Up the Courage to Say No and Walk Away   45
Lost Identity: Reclaim Your Sense of Self after Narcissistic Control   48
   Worksheet   51

PART 2: The 7 Proven Strategies for Freedom   55
CHAPTER FOUR: Know Your Limits: Defining And Enforcing Healthy Boundaries   57

Defining Your Non-Negotiables: What You Will Not Compromise On   61
Saying No without Guilt: How to Assert Your Boundaries Effectively   64
Gray Rocking and Minimal Contact: De-escalate Tension through Limited Engagement   68

CHAPTER FIVE: Healing The Inner Wound: Self-Compassion And Recovery   71

Releasing Self-Blame: Understand You Were Not the Problem   72
Practicing Forgiveness (of Yourself): Let Go of Anger and Resentment   74
Nourishing Your Soul: Strategies for Emotional and Physical Recovery   77

CHAPTER SIX: Reframing Your Narrative: Reclaiming Your Voice   80

Journaling for Insight: Processing Your Experience and Gaining Clarity — 82
Sharing Your Story: Find Comfort and Validation through Support Groups — 84
Finding Yourself Again: Rediscover Yourself, Strengths, Passions, and Purpose — 86

PART 3: Building a New Life: Thriving After Narcissistic Abuse — 90

CHAPTER SEVEN: From Isolation To Connection: Building Healthy Relationships — 92
Setting Boundaries in New Relationships: Protect Yourself from Future Manipulation — 95
Rekindling Old Connections: Reconnect with Supportive People from Your Past — 98

CHAPTER EIGHT: Prioritizing Self-Growth: Embracing Personal Development After Abuse — 101
Setting Goals and Building Dreams: Chart Your Path to a Fulfilling Future — 104
   Goal-Setting Exercise — 105
Embracing New Challenges: Step Outside Your Comfort Zone and Discovering Potential. — 106

CHAPTER NINE: Holistic Healing: Improving Your Physical And Emotional Health — 110
Nourishing Your Body, Mind, and Soul: Fueling Recovery with Food, Sleep, and Exercise — 112
   Body — 113
   Mind — 114
   Soul — 115

CHAPTER TEN: The Power Of Mindfulness And Meditation: Untethering From The Past — 117

CONCLUSION — 121

INTRODUCTION

Do you feel trapped in a relationship where your every move is scrutinized, your confidence is shattered, and your sense of self-worth is constantly attacked? You might be dealing with a narcissist.

Welcome to "How to Get Rid of a Narcissist: 7 Proven Strategies to Identify, Confront, and Free Yourself from Narcissistic Influence and Reclaim Your Health and Emotional Well-being."

Narcissists can be incredibly charming initially, drawing you in with their charisma and flattery. But beneath that appealing surface lies a manipulative, self-centered individual who thrives on controlling and diminishing others. The emotional and psychological toll they take on their victims can be profound, leaving you feeling lost, anxious, and unsure of yourself. This book guides you to breaking free from their toxic grip and reclaiming your life.

Why did I write this book? Because too many people suffer in silence, trapped in the manipulative cycles of narcissistic abuse. The damage inflicted by a narcissist can be overwhelming, but you don't have to endure it alone or without guidance. This book offers the clarity and tools you need to recognize, confront, and remove a narcissist from your life.

Understanding the nature of narcissism is the first step to regaining control. We'll explore how to spot the signs of narcissistic behavior, recognize the manipulative tactics they use, and understand the impact of their abuse on your mental and physical health. You'll gain insight into the dynamics of narcissistic relationships and learn why it's crucial to break free.

Once you understand the enemy you're dealing with, the next step is taking action. This book provides you with seven proven strategies to set boundaries, protect yourself, and begin the healing process. From asserting your boundaries to building a new life, these strategies are designed to empower you and restore your sense of self-worth.

Healing from narcissistic abuse is a journey. It involves rebuilding your identity, nurturing your emotional and physical well-being, and finding your voice again. You'll learn how to process your experiences, find support, and rediscover your strengths and passions. This journey is about more than just surviving; it's about thriving and creating a fulfilling life beyond the reach of a narcissist.

You deserve to live free from manipulation and control. The purpose of this book is to lead you through each stage of the process, providing practical tips, assistance, and motivation. Together, we will chart the path to freedom, helping you reclaim your health, happiness, and peace of mind.

Ready to start? Let's go.

PART 1:
Understanding The Narcissist

"He's such a narcissist."

"She's so narcissistic."

These are phrases you've likely heard someone you know say about another person. You might have even said it yourself at some point. A narcissistic personality has become a symbol of everything wrong with the modern world. The term "narcissist" has been thrown around a lot, and it has become significantly popular since the inception of social media.

Narcissist. Narcissism. Narcissistic. These words are hot on people's lips, but how many know what they mean and why they are problematic?

My understanding of these concepts is more technical. Psychologically, "narcissist/narcissism" is used from a diagnostic perspective to describe anyone with Narcissistic Personality Disorder. The term is derived from self-psychology, a field of psychology study. Therefore, I'm always hesitant to use it casually when I think about an individual behaving badly. Still, we'll start there.

Suppose you want to know if someone in your life is a narcissist. In that case, this person has probably treated you badly, maybe repeatedly. But how can you be sure if they're just an asshole or their behaviors can be classified as narcissistic?

Generally, therapists understand their patients and subjects only through diagnosis criteria. They use this to give behavior meaning by classifying the subjects' experiences in a way that allows them to make sense of their trauma and how this trauma informs their perception of themselves and the world. This means that therapists have a system for understanding their patients, enabling them to see not just the symptoms (behaviors) but also the causes.

So, in the first part of this book, I will be taking you on a journey to understand the narcissist. I will show you how to make sense of narcissism and narcissistic behavior.

From my experience of everyday conversations about narcissism, it's clear that people have different ideas of what narcissism is and who it describes. Of course, not having a clear idea of what something is can be confusing.

The average person will throw the word "narcissist" at anyone who obsesses over their looks or spends a little too much time investing in their appearance. Everyone is capable of becoming self-absorbed in specific situations, but true narcissism is worlds apart from this.

In the first chapter, I will take you on a journey to unmask the narcissist. You will find out who a narcissist is, the different faces they wear, the narcissistic abuse cycle, their favorite manipulation techniques, and how a narcissistic relationship pans out.

Then, in the second chapter, you will find out all about the impact narcissistic abuse can have on you. One by one, we will explore the main effects of falling victim to a narcissist – including a lost identity, shattered self-esteem, and the psychological and physical symptoms narcissistic abuse may inflict on your mind and body.

Finally, in the last chapter of this part, I will show you how to break free from the narcissist's insidious web.

As we begin this first part, prepare to be shocked at just how much a true narcissist differs from everything pop culture would have you believe.

CHAPTER ONE:
Unmasking the Narc:
Recognize the Signs and Traits

"Is my partner a narcissist?"

I get this question A LOT from people, mostly women, trying to make sense of their partners' crazy behavior. And I know why – these people need something concrete to explain the reality they're living in their relationships.

Since you're reading this, you can relate to them. Maybe you have a partner who tells you everything you do is wrong. Or perhaps it's your mother – she makes you feel guilty when you decline to do something she wants. Or maybe a friend constantly twists your words and uses them against you.

Here you are, searching for answers – and that tells me you already know there's something amiss with this person. But you're unsure of what they are... Are they a narcissist, a sociopath, or just abusive? What are they?

So many people want this information. If you're trying to determine why that person in your life behaves the way they do, this chapter will help you with an unofficial diagnosis to have all the validation necessary to truly understand your experience. And then, you will be able to move on.

Over the past decade, there has been a rise in materialism, cultural entitlement, and antisocial behavior in society. Some believe there's an epidemic of narcissism. You may think of narcissism as extreme self-involvement. This means investing more mental and emotional energy than is appropriate for oneself. It means being overly focused on one's feelings, needs, and desires at others' expense.

In the beginning, experts didn't think narcissism could be pathological. Rather, it was considered a response to developmental issues in childhood. For instance – infants and young children focus on their needs and desires above all else by default. At that stage, they are incapable of understanding the feelings and perspectives of others.

Problems typically arise when natural defense mechanisms become fixed and rigid. Defense mechanisms are akin to tricks that the mind conjures to protect a person from discomfort, anxiety, and emotional pain. They develop automatically to help us cope with difficult feelings or situations. Think of them as shields for distressing emotions.

Although it's a normal trait, narcissism can become pathological or destructive. For a narcissist, defense mechanisms like idealization provide them with a sense of uniqueness to combat fragmentation and feelings of shame and humiliation.

During my research process for this book, I learned that the term "narcissist" is quite layered. The diagnosis of narcissism itself is nuanced. To understand who a narcissist is, you must first know that the term encompasses a wide spectrum of behaviors, ranging from individuals with mild narcissistic traits to those with full-blow Narcissistic Personality Disorder (NPD).

On the narcissism spectrum, we have benign narcissists – those who are self-centered but not as harmful. Then, we have insidious narcissists who will exploit and harm others for personal gain. It's safe to say that everyone on this spectrum is a "narcissist" in their own way. However, for a person to be diagnosed with NPD or classified as a "true narcissist," they must meet five or more of the nine criteria for narcissism as recognized in the DSM-5.

Based on current information, NPD may be defined as a "pervasive pattern of grandiosity (in fantasy or behavior), need for admiration, and lack of empathy, beginning by early adulthood and present in a variety of contexts."

People with NPD are often deeply infatuated with themselves. Those around them exist to echo their self-admiration. Similar to audiences being instructed to applaud, the people around a pathological narcissist have one role: to applaud nonstop and serve as mirrors reflecting the narcissist's magnificence.

These are the traits that also double as the criteria for officially or unofficially diagnosing a person with NPD:

1. **Grandiose sense of self-importance**: The narcissist believes that their presence and contribution are pivotal to the success, happiness, or equilibrium of others and any relationships or ventures they're involved in. *"The project would have failed without my help. They needed me." "If it weren't for my help, who knows where you would have ended up!"*

2. **Preoccupation with fantasies of beauty, intelligence, power, unlimited success, or ideal love**: The narcissist believes they are capable of extraordinary achievement even when their skills and abilities don't point to this happening. *"If I get hired, I will soon be running the place." "I will win the Miss World pageant and become famous beyond imagination. Wait and see!"*

3. **Need for excessive admiration**: The narcissist doesn't want the ordinary compliments people offer as a normal part of interaction. Instead, they want others to admire their looks, skills, accomplishments, or existence. They feed on admiration from others, so they need it constantly. *"Isn't it remarkable how this dress sets off my eye colors?"* Boasting and bragging come naturally to the narcissist, and they recount compliments and praises as much as possible to remind others of their "superiority."

4. **A belief that they are special and unique and can only associate with other special people**: Do you know that one person who's always quick to pull the "I want to talk to your supervisor" card? That's what being a narcissist is like. The narcissist firmly believes they should only have to deal with high-status and top-level people like them. They work hard to infiltrate high-status cliques, social groups, and meetings even when unwanted. *"Yes, I went to college with the new director; we're great friends." "I will set up a meeting with the CEO to let him know my thoughts on the company's new directives."*
5. **Sense of entitlement**: The narcissist believes that success should take hard work-but not for them. They believe they should always have the nicest things-the biggest room, the best seat, the top score, the best tickets—because they're special and superior to everyone else. They may not say it aloud, but their actions and behaviors will communicate this sense of entitlement.
6. **Lack of empathy**: This is a cold inability to understand other people's feelings. The narcissist lacks emotional awareness and depth. It's not just that they don't "care" about anyone else's feelings; they don't even know these feelings exist. To them, they are the only ones capable of feeling a certain way.
7. **Exploitative behavior**: To the narcissist, everyone else is a tool. They don't see people as individuals with feelings, needs, and desires, which is parallel to their lack of awareness. Everything they do is in their own selfish interest, and they don't feel guilty for taking advantage of others to serve their interests.
8. **Envy**. The narcissist may be envious of others or believe that they're jealous of them. They constantly compare themselves to others, wishing they had these people's success. So, they falsely believe that others envy them to maintain their ego

and faux sense of superiority. Their ego couldn't handle being perceived as "normal" or "average."

"Everyone knows when I enter a room. They know they'll never be as beautiful as me."

9. **Arrogant attitude**. Arrogance and conceit are the first traits people notice in narcissists, which is why anyone arrogant or haughty may be wrongly perceived as a narcissist. This attitude reflects how the narcissist disregards others' rights or positions and demands that other people bend to their will. They will cut in lines, patronize others, and behave as though they are entitled to what belongs to someone else rightfully.

If someone in your life appears to have less interest in you (and your relationship) than they do in themselves, take as much time as needed to evaluate these nine markers of NPD objectively. Not everyone is self-absorbed or incapable of forming authentic interpersonal connections. But if you know anyone with five or more of these traits, then they are most likely somewhere on the narcissism spectrum.

Two Faces of the Narcissist: Grandiose and Vulnerable Narcissistic Types

Remember the phrase, "Mirror, mirror on the wall, who's the fairest of them all?" It was famously uttered in the fairy tale Snow White. Culturally, we use this line as a symbolic representation of narcissism. It displays the classic narcissistic traits explained above—excessive self-absorption, need for validation, comparison/competition with others, insecurity, and a lack of empathy. Snow White itself is a cautionary tale that highlights the negative consequences of pathological narcissism, as displayed in the character of the Evil Queen.

We all need a certain degree of narcissism for a healthy personality. It gives us adequate self-esteem so that we can thrive and pursue goals and interests in our personal and professional lives. Too little narcissism can make us feel unworthy, unlovable, and inadequate. Too much can turn us into grandiose exhibitionists who disregard everyone else.

I mentioned earlier that narcissism is nuanced, and it exists on a spectrum. This means that narcissistic traits can manifest differently in people with NPD.

Recently, psychologists have started to focus on these differences as a way of classifying narcissists. Until recent years, discussions around narcissists centered on the extroverted, arrogant individuals who come off as "grandiose." But in research and therapy sessions, psychotherapists had clients who were more aptly described as "vulnerable" than grandiose. Thus, this conflicted with the traditional understanding of narcissists.

Consequently, experts addressed these discrepancies by including both grandiose and vulnerable manifestations of narcissism to achieve a more well-rounded view of the big picture. Both terms accurately depict narcissists but couldn't be described by a singular term.

The "two faces" of narcissism are grandiose and vulnerable. They both represent related but different traits. Grandiose narcissism, for example, is marked by arrogance, boldness, confidence, and high self-esteem relating to their ego and disagreeableness. Conversely, vulnerable narcissism is marked by anxiety, low self-esteem, and low confidence, which also relate to ego-centric and insensitive behaviors.

As an illustration, let's consider the three individuals below and their personality traits:

1. Your favorite TikTok influencer constantly makes videos about the celebrities she knows and the high-status places she can access. From the way she name-drops, it's obvious that she thinks highly of herself. You can tell she feels superior to others, especially her followers. Every conversation is an opportunity to share her life experiences, regardless of the subject. She believes the world revolves around her. But she's charming, attractive, and quite funny. You like her a lot despite her self-absorbed behavior. You wish you could be friends.
2. Your introverted and shy friend would be more accurately described as an acquaintance. You've tried hard but can't seem to get through his shell. He is often sad but also full of himself. He always wants things done his way. People describe him as rigid. He's rarely compassionate toward others and constantly complains about them. His main complaints focus on how no one appreciates his brilliance or skill. You and other friends have tried talking to him about his sadness, but he refuses to accept responsibility. Instead, he tells you everything would be fine if others recognized his intelligence.
3. Your colleague at work constantly brags about career-related accomplishments on Twitter and LinkedIn. However, you disagree with him on how great they are. He puts down other colleagues and never expresses gratitude when a coworker helps him. He demands special treatment, and he becomes mean and vindictive when he doesn't receive it. He's also quite defensive when critiqued. But your boss thinks he's a "go-getter." You think he's a suck-up.

All three individuals display traits of narcissism. The first person, extroverted and charming, is what we call a grandiose narcissist. The second, insecure but entitled, is considered a vulnerable narcissist.

The third, arrogant and defensive, combines grandiose and vulnerable.

When you hear the word "narcissist," you likely think of the grandiose type. They're outgoing, confident, and bold, so chances of seeing them at work and in relationships are high. They draw you in with their charm, but eventually, you meet their self-centered and callous side. Vulnerable narcissists are harder to recognize because they're typically introverted, depressed, and sensitive to criticism. Still, they are just as self-centered and callous as their grandiose peers.

Grandiose Narcissist

Also called the overt or exhibitionist narcissist, the grandiose narcissist is charming, funny, attractive, and controlling. Their nature is such that they typically have success, wealth, and fame. This individual spends their life pursuing admiration, praise, and perfection. They have a nasty sense of entitlement and become enraged by criticism.

Outwardly, the grandiose narcissist looks pretty good and normal. But when you take a closer look, you will see glimpses of worthlessness, inadequacy, envy, rejection, and rage beneath their facade of superiority. This person sees others as mere objects to enhance their perception. You become useless to them as soon as you can no longer fulfill that function. And what do they do? They devalue and discard.

Vulnerable Narcissist

The vulnerable narcissist may also be referred to as the covert or closet narcissist. This personality type can be deceiving because you won't even recognize them as a narcissist unless you're sufficiently informed about narcissism and NPD.

Unlike the grandiose individual, the vulnerable narcissist doesn't invest emotionally in the self. Rather, their emotional investment goes toward the omnipotent. In other words, this person enhances their self-perception by putting others on a pedestal. They need others' approval and set unrealistic standards to portray themselves as exceptional.

Whereas the exhibitionist says, "I must be perfect to feel alright," the closet says, "The more beauty, power, riches, and fame I have, the better I will feel."

NPD develops in response to parental rejection and devaluation, as well as an emotionally invalidating environment. Parents of narcissists are either cold and dismissive, or they interact with their kids to meet their own needs, such as setting unrealistic expectations and standards to assuage inner feelings of unworthiness.

Grandiose: When a parent uses their child as a proxy to feel better and boost their ego, this affects the child significantly. The parent projects high expectations and treats the child as though they're special and better than others. In return, the child enjoys the admiration and adoration because they feel good.

The catch is that the child's true feelings, thoughts, and needs are dismissed and pushed aside. Consequently, the child only portrays a version of themselves that matches the parent's expectations and standards. This is usually a confident, brilliant, and successful version. If they ever show a version of their true self that differs from what the parents expect, they are faced with disapproval, criticism, embarrassment, and shame.

So, even though these children appear loved and adored on the surface, they are merely tools for the parents to feel good about themselves. The child becomes a mirror of their parent's needs and desires and is never loved or accepted for who they truly are.

Vulnerable: Compared to the grandiose type, children who develop the vulnerable form of narcissism are raised in an environment where they are met with subtle or clear criticism for just being themselves. They are treated badly, spoken to hurtfully, and made to feel unimportant as kids. Often, these kids respond with extreme modesty. They may avoid calling attention to their abilities and talents to please their parents. They usually dismiss their needs and feelings to satisfy their parents.

In short, vulnerable narcissists feel like they must hide their true selves as a result of being made to feel unimportant and ashamed in childhood.

The bottom line is that narcissism manifests primarily in these two ways.

Love Bombing and Devaluing: Deciphering the Narcissistic Cycle of Abuse

Love bombing. You probably know it from reading about it on the internet. Love bombing is a form of manipulation used to pull in a potential unsuspecting victim in the early phase of a relationship with the narcissist. It involves flooding this person with flattery, gifts, and overt displays of affection. It is intense and captivating.

In this beginning stage, you may wonder how the narcissist seems to know you so well in only a short period. Or, in a romantic sense, you might feel like you've known them all your life even though you met two weeks ago.

To draw you in and elicit such strong feelings, the narcissist might charm you with a faux personality. They might lie about their interests to come across as your compatible match. Being love-bombed can be quite gripping. It feels magical – something out of a fairy tale. You may feel like you've finally met your soul mate or twin flame.

When the narcissist love bombs you, the world may feel like a different place. Flowers look more vibrant, music sounds sweeter, the sky seems brighter, and you feel SEEN. The narcissist idealizes, worships, and enchants you. The experience is truly amazing, but unfortunately, it's all a farce.

Love bombing is the narcissist's way of locking you in, getting you hooked, and ensuring you become enamored with the relationship (and them). It lays the foundation for getting all the admiration, affection, and validation they need from you. You think they're sweet and vulnerable, but it's a facade to draw you in. And they do it with the information you offer up unknowingly.

Falling in love, in general, is an intense experience. The honeymoon phase is often enjoyable and memorable. You are giddy and excited to deeply connect with this new person, to become vulnerable with them and vice versa, and to become intimate. You're also eager to evaluate compatibility by being honest with each other about your likes and dislikes.

Yes, falling in love feels euphoric – like you're on a high – but it isn't a fabrication. Love bombing is, and it often kickstarts the narcissistic abuse cycle.

The "narcissistic abuse cycle" refers to a pattern of behavior exhibited by narcissists in the context of romantic relationships.

This cycle begins with idealization, where the narcissist places you on a pedestal and establishes a deep sense of connection. They do this by showering you with intense attention and affection to form a strong bond within days of meeting.

During the idealization phase, the narcissist may buy lavish gifts, make grand romantic gestures, or talk about your future together to make you feel special. They use whatever method they think will appeal to you the most.

The narcissist's goal is to establish a sense of deep connection and dependency to make you susceptible to manipulation and control as your relationship progresses. It can be difficult to see through the potential manipulation due to the narcissist's charming and seductive nature.

How long this phase lasts is determined by various tactics, such as your personality, the narcissist's tactics, and the unique circumstances of your relationship. It is usually short-lived, though. From reports, it lasts anywhere from a few weeks to a few months. In some cases, it can even last up to a whole year. According to a survey of 500 individuals who have been love-bombed by narcissists, the average duration is 5 ½ months for narcissistic men and 3 ½ months for narcissistic women. The max duration was six months.

The narcissist will use love bombing to establish an instant emotional connection and gain control over you. Once this is achieved and you are attached and dependent on them, they gradually begin transitioning to the devaluation phase, where their true self manifests.

As the relationship progresses, after love bombing comes devaluing.

The "devaluation" phase is when things start to change dramatically. The narcissist replaces over-the-top affection and attention with more negative behaviors. They become dismissive, critical, and emotionally abusive. They may even become physically abusive. At the same time, the narcissist employs gaslighting, projection, blame-shifting, and other manipulation tactics to control your feelings and actions.

Everything that drew you to them in the love bombing phase disappears, and you start to feel alone and unloved. The abrupt shift in behavior can leave you feeling confused and deeply hurt, especially as you struggle to understand what went wrong with the relationship.

Now, there's usually another phase: Discard.

When the narcissist no longer sees you as valuable, or when they meet a new source of validation, they will discard you with urgency. In the discard phase, they abruptly end the relationship or become emotionally distant to force you to end it.

In some cases, the narcissist might "hoover," which is when they try to draw you back in after discarding you. They will make grand promises, guilt-trip you, or use love bombing to gain your attention and affection again.

So, how do you know if you're being love-bombed?

Watch out for these signs:

- Showering you with compliments, attention, and intense affection as soon as you meet
- Talking to you about deep commitment, future plans, and spending forever together within a short period of the meeting.
- Staying in constant communication through texts, social media, and calls.
- Saying you're the best thing to ever happen to them.
- Displaying signs of possessiveness and extreme jealousy.
- Lavishing you with extravagant gifts and outings and grand romantic gestures.

When being love-bombed, consider your thoughts, feelings, and responses. Some things to notice include:

- Experience intense highs and lows emotionally
- Feeling overwhelmed or smothered
- Spending less time with loved ones
- Feeling pressured to spend all of your time with them or reply to messages immediately
- Feeling obligated to commit to the relationship even though it's early
- Becoming dependent on them emotionally, financially, etc

- Adopting their interests, values, and habits
- Changing yourself to meet their expectations

When a love bombing abruptly ends, it increases anxiety. Unfortunately, devaluation comes next. When it happens, the relationship becomes an addictive cycle where you're constantly trying to get back to the love-bombing phase. Even as the narcissist abuses and devalues you, you cling to memories of the love bombing phase due to how good it felt.

Gaslighting and Projection: Unmasking the Narcissist's Favorite Manipulation Tactics

Having a narcissistic partner is like going on a rollercoaster ride. The relationship begins like a fairy tale, only to transform into your worst nightmare. It's possible for anyone to find themselves in a relationship with a narcissist. Still, the most susceptible are those with a history of emotional abuse and trauma. They are predisposed to getting trapped in a relationship with narcissistic dynamics.

The number one reason why narcissists can trap their victims in the abuse cycle is their toolkit of manipulation tactics. When you meet a pathological narcissist, manipulation kick starts in the honeymoon phase of your relationship. Subsequently, the narcissist employs gaslighting, projection, and other tactics to undermine your self-worth and confidence. This creates a constant cycle of devastating emotional abuse.

You should know that narcissists don't manipulate you out of a lack of understanding of the suffering they're inflicting on you. Rather, they are incapable of empathizing or feeling remorse for their actions. They will always avoid taking accountability for what they have done. They will much rather blame you for everything that goes wrong in the relationship.

Gaslighting

Individuals with NPD use gaslighting as a tool for controlling and dominating others. Gaslighting occurs when a person distorts, alters, or denies something that happened to make you doubt your thoughts, feelings, memories, perception of reality, and sanity.

The narcissist uses gaslighting to undermine your self-worth, confidence, and sense of what's real. They do this to make you dependent on their version of reality, which gives them power over you. They may derive a sense of control, enjoyment, and satisfaction from creating doubt, confusion, and distress in your head.

According to psychoanalists, there's something called the Gaslight Effect. This refers to the psychological impact of gaslighting on emotional and mental well-being. The Gaslight Effect involves three phases:

1. **Disbelief**: This is the initial phase when the narcissist gradually starts to gaslight you. In this phase, you experience doubt and confusion but find it hard to believe that someone who cares about you would deliberately twist the facts of a situation. You may question your memory and judgment or rationalize it with, "I probably misunderstood them." Victims often brush it off as a coincidence or a one-time occurrence.
2. **Defense**: As the gaslighting advances, you enter the defense phase. This is where you seek evidence and offer explanations to make sense of what's happening. You might even confront the narcissist about their behavior because you desperately want to protect your sanity.
3. **Depression**: If the gaslighting continues, you will enter a state of depression. The constant self-doubt and questioning can stir feelings of emotional exhaustion, isolation, and helplessness. You may feel detached from reality and become wary of your emotions and perceptions.

To gaslight you, the narcissist may employ the following phrases:

- **"You're overreacting"**: This dismisses your feelings and makes you question their validity.
- **"I never said/did that"**: The narcissist denies previous conversations, actions, or promises to reinforce your self-doubt.
- **"You're the one always causing issues for me."** They blame you for the disagreements and conflicts in the relationship. This makes you feel responsible for what goes wrong.
- **"You have it wrong"**: They outright deny something you clearly remember, making you question your memory.
- **"You're always trying to start a fight"**: This phrase shifts the focus from their actions to you. It is used for deflection.

Gaslighting often has profound and damaging effects, which we will explore in-depth in the next chapter.

Projection

As you now know, narcissists typically lack self-awareness. Their sense of self-perception generally depends on the other. In other words, how they see themselves depends on how others see them. They have a penchant for denying personal flaws and blaming others for their mistakes, shortcomings, and misfortunes. In psychology, we call this Projection, and it's a handy manipulation tactic narcissists use.

Projection is when a person sees their negative traits and behaviors in others. Anyone who's ever been on the receiving end of a narcissist's projections knows it can be incredibly frustrating. They accuse you of things with zero basis. They criticize you for behaving in ways they're guilty of. All of this is a projection. The narcissist uses projection as a defense mechanism to shift blame and avoid feeling guilt. They might accuse you of being unfaithful, claim you hate them, or even call you a narcissist.

Keep in mind that we all project from time to time. For example, someone insecure may make fun of another person for the same thing they are insecure about. But compared to the average person, the narcissist projects much more frequently and on a bigger scale.

Projection occurs subconsciously, meaning that the narcissist may genuinely believe that the things they're attributing to you originate from you. It serves different purposes, such as:

- **Avoiding responsibilities and mistakes**. The narcissist may project their shortcomings onto you to avoid taking responsibility. They also do it to preserve the illusion of being flawless. Since they consider themselves superior and perfect, they attribute their undesirable qualities to you so that they can seem faultless in comparison. For example, if you confront them about dishonesty, they may accuse you of lying. If they envy your success, they may accuse you of jealousy.
- **Shifting blame**. When confronted about their behaviors, actions, or mistakes, narcissists will shift the blame to you or someone else. This means they can evade responsibility, control how you perceive them, and maintain the power in your relationship.
- **Eroding your self-esteem**. The narcissist manipulates and controls your emotions by projecting their insecurities on you. The constant blame, criticism, and accusations can slowly diminish your self-esteem, making you more vulnerable to further manipulation.

The best way to handle narcissistic projection is to constantly remind yourself that it's nothing but a reflection of how the narcissist feels about themselves. Nothing they say is grounded in reality. They never paint an accurate picture. And you're the only one who defines yourself.

So far, we've unmasked the narcissists by exploring what they are, the faces they wear, and the manipulation tactics they employ to keep you subjugated and trapped in the narcissistic abuse cycle.

Now, it's time to discuss how the abuse may impact you. How does being in a relationship with a narcissist affect the mind and body?

Let's find out in the next chapter!

CHAPTER TWO:
Narcissistic Victim Syndrome: The Impact Of Narcissistic Abuse

Let me tell you about Jane. Everyone instantly liked her-friendly, smart, and always ready with a smile. Jane was in a relationship with Mark for five years. At first, everything seemed perfect. Mark was charming and attentive. He made Jane feel like she was the center of his world. But as time went on, his true colors started to show. Mark was a classic narcissist.

It started with small, subtle criticisms. He'd comment on her appearance, suggesting she'd look better if she dressed a certain way or lost a little weight. Though seemingly harmless, these comments began to plant doubt in Jane's mind.

As the months passed, Mark's criticisms became more frequent and personal. He'd undermine her accomplishments, making her feel insignificant. If Jane shared a success at work, Mark would downplay it, saying things like, "Anyone could have done that," or "It's not a big deal." This constant belittling chipped away at Jane's self-esteem. She started to doubt her abilities and question her worth.

Mark's behavior wasn't limited to just criticisms. He'd also manipulate situations to make Jane feel guilty or responsible for his unhappiness. It was somehow Jane's fault if he was in a bad mood. If something went wrong, Jane was to blame. This kind of emotional manipulation made Jane constantly second-guess herself. She became hyper-aware of Mark's moods, trying to anticipate his reactions and avoid triggering his anger or disappointment.

As you know, isolation is another hallmark of narcissistic abuse, and Jane experienced this firsthand. Mark would get jealous whenever Jane spent time with her friends or family. He'd accuse her of not caring about him or being selfish. To keep the peace, Jane started to withdraw from her social circle. She stopped attending gatherings and reduced her interactions with friends. Over time, she felt increasingly isolated and alone, with Mark being her only significant relationship.

The isolation made Jane more dependent on Mark, which only intensified the abuse. Without the support of friends and family, Jane felt trapped. She didn't have anyone to turn to, and Mark's voice became the dominant narrative in her life. He'd tell her she was lucky to have him, that no one else would put up with her. Jane started to believe him.

This cycle of abuse led to what's known as narcissistic victim syndrome. Jane experienced symptoms like anxiety, depression, and a pervasive sense of worthlessness. Physical symptoms also emerged. Jane had trouble sleeping, often lying awake, replaying arguments, or worrying about the next confrontation. She experienced frequent headaches and stomach issues, signs of the chronic stress she was under. Her body was in a constant state of fight-or-flight, which took a toll on her health.

Despite all this, Jane couldn't bring herself to leave Mark. The psychological manipulation had created a trauma bond, a deep emotional attachment to her abuser. Jane felt conflicted, torn between her love for Mark and the realization that his behavior was destroying her. She often blamed herself for the problems in the relationship, thinking that if she could be better or do things differently, Mark would change.

It took a long time for Jane to recognize the extent of the abuse and its impact on her. When she finally did, a lightbulb went off in her head. She realized she wasn't the problem; Mark was. Jane started to understand his behavior patterns and how they had affected her. That realization was the first step in her journey to recovery.

Picture this: You were in a relationship where your entire reality has been twisted and distorted. The person whom you believe was in love with you has mercilessly manipulated, gaslighted, ridiculed, devalued, and violated you. You thought you knew this person, but it was all an illusion. And now that illusion has shattered into thousands of little fragments.

This person idealized and put you on a pedestal. Then, they violently shoved you off that pedestal. They devalued you so much that your sense of self is no more. It's been diminished and eroded by their actions. At some point, this person even discarded you over and over. They would push you away only to lure you back into the cycle. Perhaps they even stalked, harassed, and bullied you to stay in the relationship.

This was no healthy relationship. It was a covert and insidious assault on your psyche and sense of security in yourself and the world. Now that it's over, you don't have obvious scars, but there are fractured memories, broken pieces, and inner wounds.

This is how narcissistic abuse works.

Narcissists can use verbal and emotional abuse, gaslighting, projection, triangulation, stonewalling, smear campaigns, sabotage, and tons of other tactics to coerce and control their victims in an intimate relationship.

The abuse is chronic, and as a result, victims often struggle with various psychological and physiological symptoms during the relationship and long after it's over. In many cases, victims may even develop what psychologists call "Narcissistic Victim Syndrome," depending on the duration and intensity of the abusive relationship.

Narcissistic victim syndrome may also be referred to as narcissistic abuse syndrome. The term collectively describes the specific and severe effects of a narcissistic relationship dynamic. Although it is not formally acknowledged as a mental health issue, there's a consensus that narcissistic abuse can have a serious, long-term impact on physical and psychological health.

It's often difficult to pinpoint or label exactly what's happening in the middle of an ongoing abuse cycle. Narcissistic individuals are skilled at distorting reality to align with their own self-serving purposes. They are also adept at using love bombing to win their victims over after clear incidents of abuse. Some even brainwash their victims into accepting that they're the abusive ones. That's how insidious narcissistic abuse can be.

Suppose you suspect that you're in a dysfunctional relationship with a narcissist but don't know for sure. In that case, I will help you recognize how the abuse cycle may have changed your life for the worse. We will explore the physical, emotional, mental, and psychological effects of narcissistic abuse one by one. By the end, you will be able to tell whether you're suffering from narcissistic victim syndrome or not.

Emotional and Mental Impact: Recognize the Signs of Anxiety, Depression, and PTSD

In a relationship with a narcissistic partner, the narcissist will do so many things that leave you feeling and acting unstable. Then, they will tag you "crazy" and make sure everyone knows it. Narcissistic abuse impairs your sense of self, reality, and emotional security. It's even worse because there's usually no physical abuse, though there might be in some cases. If it goes on for long enough, narcissistic abuse can have a severe mental and emotional impact.

The pattern of controlling and manipulative behavior exhibited by narcissists can lead to anxiety, depression, and PTSD in victims. So, you must know the signs that these mental health issues may be manifesting in your life. This is vital for healing and recovery.

Anxiety

Relationships with a narcissistic dynamic are marked by unpredictability and constant tension. The narcissist's behavior creates an atmosphere of fear and uncertainty. Consequently, you find yourself constantly feeling anxious about their moods and reactions. This may manifest in the following ways:

- **Constant worry**: If you live or work for someone who always criticizes you at random and belittles your efforts, it can lead to nonstop worry. You might constantly worry about your actions and their potential reactions. You might second-guess yourself to try and preempt their next outburst. This relentless self-monitoring will eventually make you chronically anxious.
- **Hypervigilance**: Having a romantic partner who uses gaslighting techniques can put you in hypervigilance. For example, suppose this person repeatedly accuses you of making stuff up even though they did the things you confronted them about. In that case, you might start doubting your memory. In turn, this can make you become hyper-alert to every detail of your interactions. It means you constantly live on the edge.

Anxiety manifests beyond the mind. It can cause physical symptoms, such as stomachaches, headaches, and a racing heart. Imagine having to deal with a headache or racing heart all the time. You will, of course, find it hard to relax and focus on things that matter.

Depression

Narcissistic abuse can also cause depression in victims. The frequent manipulation and devaluation diminish a person's sense of self-worth, which triggers a persistent state of hopelessness. The signs often include:

- **Chronic sadness**: When your partner never fails to remind you that you aren't good enough or that you are the symbol

of what's wrong with your relationship, you will subconsciously internalize these negative messages. Over time, it can lead to a deep, pervasive sadness. This sadness can be compounded by the belief that your situation might never change.
- **Loss of interest**: You may no longer enjoy your favorite activities. The things you love will no longer bring you happiness, as the narcissist's voice echoes in your mind, undermining your pleasure.
- **Fatigue**: Depression saps a person's energy and strength. It makes you feel like getting through the day is impossible. The narcissist's unrealistic expectations and the walking on eggshells drain you of life, leaving you emotionally exhausted at all times.

Post-Traumatic Stress Disorder (PTSD)

Depending on the duration and intensity, narcissistic abuse can be so severe that it leads to PTSD. For example, you're more likely to experience PSTD or C-PSTD if you grew up with an abusive, narcissistic parent. The unpredictable and chronic nature of the abuse engineer an environment where you feel constantly threatened.

Signs of narcissistic abuse-induced PTSD include:
- **Flashbacks**: PTSD often involves reliving traumatic experiences. For example, if a narcissistic parent constantly humiliates you in front of others, you might experience flashbacks during social situations, feeling the same shame and fear as if it were happening again.
- **Nightmares**: The trauma of narcissistic abuse can invade your sleep. Imagine frequently dreaming about past abusive incidents, waking up in a sweat, and feeling just as trapped and helpless as you did during the actual events.

- **Avoidance**: People with PTSD often avoid triggers associated with their trauma. If you've left an abusive relationship, you might find yourself avoiding places you used to go with your abuser or steering clear of conversations about relationships altogether, fearing they might bring up painful memories.
- **Hyperarousal**: This symptom includes being easily startled, having trouble sleeping, or feeling irritable. For instance, you might jump at loud noises, have difficulty falling asleep because your mind is racing with thoughts about past abuse, or snap at others because your nerves are constantly on edge.

It's important to understand how narcissistic abuse can lead to these mental health problems. As I said, you need the knowledge to start recovering from the aftermath of narcissistic abuse.

Physical Impact: The Toll of Narcissistic Abuse on Your Body

When you've been entrapped in the narcissistic abuse cycle for a significant time, it gets to a point where your body remains stuck in survival mode. Not living or thriving – just existing. At this stage, nothing the narcissist does or says shocks you anymore – if anything, you feel numb. You're used to being looped into a cycle of conflict and getting blamed for everything.

You're in constant mental fatigue, but now, you can feel the fatigue spreading to your body. It might feel like it's all in your head, but it isn't. Narcissistic abuse triggers chronic stress and trauma. These can manifest in your body as various dysfunctions.

The body can tell when it's under attack from stress and excessive worry. So, it maps out defense mechanisms for protection to ensure survival. This is the sympathetic nervous system at work.

As you know, the nervous system is responsible for every bodily function. The nervous system comprises the brain, spinal cord, and nerves. Our nerves carry information from the body to the brain so that the latter can take necessary action.

One part of the nervous system is the sympathetic nervous system (SNS), which is in charge of readying the body to fight emergencies and stress. When you sense a threat, the SNS triggers the production of stress hormones (cortisol, adrenaline) to inform the body. This leads to increased breathing, faster heart rate, blood pressure, sweat, expanded pupils, etc. All of this happens to send more blood toward the brain and heart.

Stress is a normal part of daily life. The kind of stress we experience from minor inconveniences is called acute stress. So, with this kind of stress, these responses work because we know how to eliminate the stressors. But when you're a victim of narcissistic abuse, stress becomes chronic, and these responses start working against you.

Being constantly exposed to stress puts your body in a permanent state of hypervigilance, which overstimulates the SNS. You might experience headaches, muscle tension, or even chest pain. Your body's stress response, often called the "fight or flight" reaction, is continuously activated. The nervous system works harder than normal to protect you, which leads to physical illness. Over time, this can wear you down, leading to fatigue and a weakened immune system. This impairs your ability to fight diseases, increasing illness.

Here are more of the physical impact of narcissistic abuse on the body:

- **Sleep Disturbances**

Have you ever been tossing and turning at night, unable to sleep because your mind is racing? That's common in victims of narcissistic abuse. Sleep disturbances are a frequent complaint. Insomnia or nightmares can become your nightly companions, making it hard for your body to recover and function properly.

- **Gastrointestinal Issues**

Your gut is surprisingly sensitive to emotional turmoil. Many people under narcissistic abuse report gastrointestinal issues like irritable bowel syndrome (IBS), nausea, or stomach pain. The constant anxiety can disrupt your digestive system, leading to these uncomfortable symptoms.

- **Cardiovascular Problems**

The constant stress from narcissistic abuse can also affect your heart. High blood pressure, rapid heart rate, and even an increased risk of heart disease are possible outcomes. Your cardiovascular system is under constant strain, which is bad for your long-term health.

- **Chronic Pain and Inflammation**

Believe it or not, narcissistic abuse can lead to chronic pain and inflammation. Conditions like fibromyalgia, where you experience widespread musculoskeletal pain, are more common in those who've been through severe emotional abuse. The stress and anxiety can cause your body to become inflamed, leading to these chronic pain conditions.

- **Weight Fluctuations**

Have you noticed changes in your weight? This could be due to the emotional toll of the abuse. Some people lose their appetite and weight due to stress and anxiety, while others might turn to food for comfort, leading to weight gain. Both extremes are unhealthy and can affect your overall well-being.

- **Immune System Suppression**

Chronic stress from narcissistic abuse can weaken your immune system. This makes you more susceptible to infections and illnesses. You might get sick more often or take longer to recover from common colds and other ailments.

- **Cognitive Impairment**

The constant gaslighting and manipulation can leave you feeling confused and mentally exhausted. This cognitive impairment isn't just in your head; it has physical repercussions. You might struggle with memory, concentration, and decision-making, making everyday tasks challenging.

- **Fatigue**

One of the most common physical symptoms is overwhelming fatigue. It's not just about feeling tired; it's an all-encompassing exhaustion that doesn't go away with rest. This fatigue can make it hard to get through your daily routine, affecting your work, relationships, and overall quality of life.

- **Skin Problems**

Your skin can also show signs of stress. Conditions like eczema, psoriasis, and acne can flare up or worsen. Stress and anxiety may result in hormonal imbalances, which manifest in these skin issues.

The physical toll of narcissistic abuse is extensive and can affect almost every part of your body. If you're experiencing any of these symptoms, it's essential to break free from the abuse cycle immediately. I will show you how to do that.

Shattered Self-Esteem and Self-Worth: How the Narcissist Assaults Your Sense of Self

Humans have six core needs. One of these is self-esteem, which is confidence in one's worth and abilities. Self-esteem instills a sense of self-respect. This is fundamental to life—it's important to feel good about yourself, to feel like you have value, and to believe that you're deserving of good things in life. Unfortunately, narcissistic abuse disrupts this core need.

Though often conflated as synonyms, self-esteem and self-worth are two different concepts. Still, they are related.

Self-esteem encompasses the thoughts and feelings you have about yourself based on personal judgments you make from moment to moment. It can change based on mood, performance, circumstance, or external validation. People who have more negative thoughts and feelings tend to have low self-esteem. They also tend to have low self-confidence.

Meanwhile, self-worth is "a broader and more stable form of self-esteem." Unlike self-esteem, self-worth is less susceptible to external factors. Whereas the former focuses on traits, skills, and accomplishments, self-worth encompasses your core beliefs about yourself. It comes from knowing and believing in your value as a person.

Core beliefs typically maintain consistency over time, so self-worth remains rigid despite your feelings, thoughts, behaviors, and experiences. Having high self-worth means you are more likely to:

- believe you're worthy and of value, no matter what's happening in your life
- feel deserving of love and respect from others
- embrace and love yourself exactly as you are
- be self-compassionate and respectful
- believe you can learn, grow, change, and improve
- accept your flaws and mistakes without threatening your identity or worth

When you're in a relationship with a narcissist, your self-esteem and self-worth both take severe hits. The way a narcissist sees a relationship is that if the other person is up, they must be down. And they want to keep themselves up at all times. The only way to do this is to make you feel small and unsure. They also need to convince you that you're of little to no value. The more they can disrupt your self-esteem and self-worth, the more secure they feel in the relationship.

So, they use gaslighting, projection, constant belittling and criticism, and emotional neglect to assault your sense of self and dominate you. If the relationship persists for long enough, you start to doubt yourself, lose confidence in your abilities, and feel like you aren't good enough. The nagging self-doubt that stems from getting gaslighted can erode your sense of self, leading to lower self-confidence.

Furthermore, even if you have high self-worth from inception, you will inevitably begin to internalize the narcissist's negative messages. *Maybe there's something wrong with me.* These negative beliefs are dangerous because they undermine your core beliefs about yourself, leading to impaired self-worth and self-esteem.

Suppose you had a narcissistic mother or father growing up, which further compounds the issue. Narcissistic parents are extremely critical, unsupportive, and emotionally abusive. They conditionalize affection so their children can earn their love and approval. They also set unrealistic expectations, which they expect you to meet at all costs. So, from the jump, kids raised by narcissistic parents already have the deeply ingrained belief that they are never enough, no matter how hard they try to be.

Consequently, these kids grow up with a fragmented sense of self. They tend to strongly fear abandonment or rejection based on chronic feelings of inadequacy. Since they learned early to push their needs aside for their parents, they might grow up to become people-pleasers with poor boundaries.

These sorts of experiences in early childhood can make you more vulnerable to narcissistic partners as an adult. The unhealthy dynamics feel familiar and comfortable. You may subconsciously recognize and gravitate toward the cycle of seeking affection and validation from a partner who withholds it. Narcissists can recognize these vulnerabilities, and they exploit them to keep the abuse cycle running.

Assaulting your sense of self allows the narcissist to exercise control and dominance over you. It lets them disrupt your need for autonomy. Making you feel bad about yourself disrupts your need to pursue competence.

In this journey of getting rid of the narcissist in your life, it's important to reclaim your sense of self and slowly rebuild your self-worth and self-esteem. Recognizing the cycle of abuse is one thing; deconstructing the internalized messages about your worth is another thing.

So, what can you do? Let's find out in the final chapter of this part.

CHAPTER THREE:
Breaking Free From The Web: Why You Need To Leave

Often, by the time you realize you're in a relationship with a narcissist, you are blindsided. After all, no one taught you to recognize narcissists…until now. Breaking up a healthy relationship is hard enough. But when you decide to leave a narcissist, you must be ready for war. It's even worse when you're in love with them. That alone can make leaving incredibly difficult despite the abuse. Yet, you must leave them ASAP.

In normal relationships with normal people, you can have reasonable discussions about unacceptable behaviors. With a narcissist, though, they will either gaslight you or promise to change per usual. They always change the goalpost while you walk on eggshells, and your sense of self gradually diminishes.

Sometimes, it will feel like a narcissist has truly changed, only for them to revert to default. The relationship takes one step forward and five steps backwards. And then they blame you for calling them out, not minding the hurt they are causing you.

Here's one thing you must accept as you prepare to walk out the door: You will never be able to hold a narcissist accountable. It's why you're entrapped in the dynamic and must leave that belief behind. You must accept that a narcissist cannot be fixed if you truly want to leave the relationship.

When you decide you've had enough, you may have become distant from your loved ones and support system members. Of course, this is the narcissist's machination. They want to ensure you can never leave unless it's on their term. There will be moments of clarity that you must hold on to tightly. Let "I must leave" resonate within you over and over. That way, you will have enough strength to shut the door and never look back.

You may have changed, but that doesn't mean the narcissist can. It's normal to put faith in the narcissist when they seek redemption because you know what it's like to turn your life around. The problem is the narcissist can't and won't change. I know many experts believe narcissists can change with therapeutic interventions, but this is not true.

For change to happen, a patient must be self-aware and willing to open up. Narcissists are inherently incapable of self-awareness or being open. There's arguably nothing they hate more than feeling vulnerable, which is what therapy requires.

Any so-called change your narcissistic partner makes will be fleeting and piecemeal. If you don't leave because they "promised" to change, I hate to say that you'll pay for it dearly. Know this: You're the only person that you must prioritize at this very moment. The narcissist has pummeled and whipped you into a shadow of yourself. Now, it's time to love and be kind toward yourself. It's time to put yourself first.

"If I leave him, doesn't that make me as bad? It is unspiritual!"

I get this a lot from women with narcissistic partners. We hold dearly in society due to the "Don't judge" maxim. The presupposition is that deciding something isn't good enough makes us bad people. But discernment doesn't make you a bad person. Being able to make necessary judgment calls is a valuable life skill. It makes you wise.

Think about it this way: Would you let it go on if it were your child or close friend in this relationship? Of course not. You would try your best to get them to see reason and get rid of the narcissist. So, that's the same thing you must do for yourself.

Stages of Change: What It Takes to Leave a Narcissist

You may be going through so much confusion and internal chaos at this point. You may feel like you can't make sense of your thoughts.

You may feel "stuck" in getting rid of the narcissist from your life forever.

These feelings are entirely normal – there's always confusion, ambivalence, fear, and pain centered around ending a relationship with someone you love. The unknown is scary, so it's important to understand what you're ready for in this aspect. It's best to leave a narcissist, but that doesn't mean you should be forced to.

This section is about helping you assess how ready you are to make this crucial change. To do this, we will use the Stages of Change Model, introduced by James Prochaska and Carlo DiClemente in the late 70's. It is helpful because it provides a clear framework of where a person may be regarding change and offers some clarity. This is important since being in a narcissistic relationship means you have no clarity of boundaries, respect, connection, mutual trust, and authentic love. You have no clarity of anything outside of what the narcissist dictates.

If you want to leave a narcissist, you must first ask yourself the following questions:

- Is there a support system (family, friends, mentors, therapist) in place to help you keep this commitment to leaving your abusive partner? This is vital because you do need a village to make it happen. Your support system must be filled with people who won't choose the narcissist over you, no matter what. Selecting people who won't be manipulated or pressured to choose sides is important.
- On a scale of 1 (not ready) to 10 (the readiest you can be), how ready are you to leave? It's normal for your answer to fluctuate when you ask this question daily. But look at the ballpark. To make a clean break, you must go at a pace that works for you. No one can make you leave until you truly feel at your readiest.

- Do you have any internal resources? Take this moment to think about a personal accomplishment and the skills you used to make it happen. List the qualities you admire in yourself. Write down the assets that make you unique and special.
- What is keeping you in the relationship? Think about what's keeping you stuck - those things getting in your way of leaving. Is it fear of abandonment? Is it stigma? Is it your inability to set and enforce boundaries? Perhaps you have a family and kids with the narcissist. Or you're afraid people will judge you. It could also be that you depend on the narcissist for your daily needs.

Now, here are the stages of change you will go through to leave a narcissist:

Stage 1: Pre-Contemplation

This first stage is where you start noticing changes in the narcissist. You see the red flags but don't want to see them. You might deny or rationalize their behaviors. Or you might try to change them by overcompensating, appeasing, and "fawning."

Do not ignore or make excuses for the red flags. Instead, be kind and gentle with yourself. Assess the risk of staying in the relationship. Your safety is paramount, whether physical or emotional.

Stage 2: Contemplation

During this stage, your eyes will open more and more to the dynamics of your relationship. You will have conflicting feelings about whether to leave or not. You might reminisce about good times and hope that things will improve.

To reach a decision, list the pros and cons of staying in the relationship. Think of how it's affecting your physical and mental health. Think about the meaningful relationships you've lost. Take inventory of everything the relationship has cost you. I guarantee the costs will outweigh the benefits by far.

Many victims remain in this stage for a long time. If you feel stuck here, be compassionate still. You're a work in progress.

Stage 3: Preparation

At this stage, you may start making minor changes in the narcissistic relationship. These could be as simple as gray-rocking the narcissist, setting boundaries, and minimizing your emotional responses to the narcissist. Be realistic about what you can do.

Stage 4: Action

Here is where you may finally take action to go "No Contact" or leave the narcissist completely. For this stage to succeed, you must create an exit plan. If there are kids involved, minimizing contact might be the best option. This stage can be scary because you're finally doing that thing you've always wanted to do. Support is crucial here because leaving your partner can be lonely and debilitating.

Stage 5: Maintenance

This stage is where you focus on slowly processing your trauma, healing, and generally being consistent with keeping the narcissist out of your life. It's a time to dig deep into rediscovering yourself and rebuilding your sense of self from scratch.

Stage 6: Relapse

I want to be a hundred percent transparent, which is why you should know that relapse will happen at some point. Don't judge or criticize yourself harshly when it does; it's all part of the process. Again, it's important to surround yourself with people who love and care about you. They are the ones who will help you through the phase and ensure you never have to suffer like that again.

Of course, in subsequent chapters, I will share the strategies you need to successfully complete each of these stages.

Facing the Fear of Abandonment: Build Up the Courage to Say No and Walk Away

People who have never found themselves in abusive relationships have a hard time wrapping their heads around the concept. Why would anyone remain in a relationship with a partner who mistreats and disrespects them constantly? Due to this misunderstanding, a lot of them lack empathy and compassion for victims of abuse. As a victim of narcissistic abuse, you have it even harder because people just don't see the abuse in such a dynamic.

The reality is that abuse is a multi-faceted and complex issue. In most cases, staying isn't about whether one wants to. There are numerous reasons why victims may find it hard to leave. Among these is the fear of abandonment.

Being human means you depend on others for survival. From birth, your survival and development are intricately linked to your caregiver's ability to feed, bathe, clothe, shelter, and care for you correctly.

Healthy development cannot occur without adequate physical and emotional care. Therefore, fear of abandonment often originates from unmet needs in childhood or adulthood.

Fear of abandonment is a powerful and deeply rooted form of anxiety. It is characterized by insecurity, codependency, and a maladaptive view of intimacy. Though not a clinical diagnosis, it is a symptom of many mood and personality disorders.

Sometimes, fear of abandonment stems from being consistently neglected or rejected in romantic relationships, which severely impairs one's self-worth and sense of security.

When you fear abandonment, you may constantly fret that your friends, family, or partner will leave you alone. The anxiety can be all-consuming to the point where it shapes your behaviors, decisions, and relationships profoundly.

In the context of a narcissistic relationship, fear of abandonment can make it hard to leave for many reasons.

Initially, the relationship dynamic causes you to become more reliant on the narcissist for validation and support. They engineer calculated moves to make you feel you can't survive without them. You may feel like you need them to feel whole. Therefore, merely thinking about ending the relationship can be terrifying.

Second, the narcissist might have isolated you from your loved ones. Maybe they convinced you they were the only ones who cared about you or that your friends and family were against you. Feeling isolated and alone can intensify the fear of abandonment. You may feel like there's no one else in your corner.

Third, narcissists use intermittent reinforcement to keep you hopeful. By this, I mean they alternate between periods of love bombing and devaluation. These occasional glimpses of love and affection create a strong emotional bond that makes you hope things will improve. But this is a psychological trap that makes leaving seem impossible.

If your self-worth and self-esteem are at an all-time low, the feelings of worthlessness and inadequacy can intensify your fear of abandonment. You might think, "If I leave, who else would want me?" This self-doubt is a major barrier to breaking free from the web of manipulation.

The longer you remain in the relationship, the higher your chances of forming a trauma bond with the narcissist. Similar to Stockholm Syndrome, a trauma bond is a deep emotional attachment that forms in abusive relationships.

One thing about the narcissistic abuse cycle is that it creates very intense highs and lows, leading to a bond that feels impossible to sever. You may feel a strange, paradoxical loyalty to the narcissist. This can further make it difficult to leave.

Other factors...

Apart from fear of abandonment, other factors may make it difficult to get up and leave. They include:

- Family expectations
- Financial obligations
- Children
- Dysfunctional thinking

Emotions to Expect

Once you decide to leave, prepare yourself for a whirlwind of emotions. It's a big step, so know that it's perfectly normal to experience all of these emotions.

- **Relief**: Finally, you're out of the toxic environment. You won't have to walk on eggshells or deal with manipulative behavior. It's like a weight has been lifted off your shoulders.
- **Fear**: Change can be scary. You might worry about the future or potential retaliation from the narcissist. This fear is natural, but remember, you're moving towards a healthier life.
- **Sadness**: Despite everything, you might still feel sad. It's okay to mourn losing what you hoped the relationship could be. Permit yourself to grieve.
- **Anger**: Anger is a powerful emotion and quite common in this situation. You might feel angry about the time you lost or how you were treated. Channel this anger into positive actions for your future.
- **Guilty**: You might question whether you did the right thing or feel guilty for leaving. It's crucial to affirm to yourself that

you are deserving of a relationship founded on mutual respect and love.
- **Confusion**: Ending a relationship with a narcissist can leave you feeling confused. Their manipulation might have blurred your perception. It takes time to see things clearly again.
- **Loneliness**: It's normal to feel lonely after leaving, especially if the narcissist isolated you from friends and family. Rebuilding your support network takes time, but it's worth it.

These emotions are part of the healing process. It's okay to feel them and seek support if needed.

Leaving a narcissist isn't as simple as just walking away, especially when fear of abandonment is at play. Believe in yourself – you can do it.

Lost Identity: Reclaim Your Sense of Self after Narcissistic Control

Your sense of self is your sense of "this is me" and "this isn't me." It comprises your core values, beliefs, memories, and experiences, all of which shape your perception of who you are. This sense of self starts forming in childhood, influenced by family, culture, and personal experiences. Over time, it evolves as you learn more about yourself through relationships, achievements, and even failures. It's your internal compass guiding your thoughts, feelings, and actions.

Usually, our sense of self develops subconsciously on its own. We don't give much thought to the process; it just falls into place. We slowly cultivate interests, dreams, and ambitions. We learn things, take jobs, and garner experiences from different activities. All this shapes who we are, what we believe, and how we express ourselves. But if we're unlucky enough to have a narcissistic parent, the story turns out differently.

Growing up with a parent who had strong narcissistic traits or being in a long-term relationship with a narcissistic partner can damage your sense of self severely. If you had a narcissistic parent, you probably never developed a sense of self in the first place. You might be unaware of this, similar to how we don't know what we're missing out on.

Having a narcissist in your life means you're constantly reminded that your views, ideas, thoughts, feelings, etc., are of no value. This can make it very difficult to discern your own identity and preferences.

Why?

Narcissistic abuse makes you hyper-focused on the narcissist and other people, so much so that your sense of who you are as an individual is poorly defined. In other words, you find it hard to describe yourself outside of the context of that relationship. You're someone's girlfriend, wife, mother, daughter, sister, brother, father...but who are you?

After being in a narcissistic relationship for some time, you lose touch with who you are. Your identity becomes blurred, and you might find yourself living to please the narcissist instead of being true to yourself. Your likes, dislikes, needs, wants, desires and values become synonymous with those of the narcissist. As a result, you can't define who you are and what you want, need, or desire.

If you've been in a narcissistic parent-child dynamic from early childhood, then you've probably always placed a low value on your worth. Take a moment to try and define what you like and don't like, and it'll probably circle back to what you can do for the narcissist in your life and others.

You may not even realize this until someone calls your attention or you leave the situation and don't know what to do with yourself.

One reason why narcissistic abuse is so insidious is that it doesn't strip away your identity in one night. Rather, the narcissist slowly chips away at it until every thought, word, and action from you is a mirror of theirs.

The good news is that no matter how long you've had a narcissist controlling your life, you can still absolutely develop a strong sense of self. You'll have to put in time and effort, but it is possible.

Reclaiming your sense of self involves reframing your thoughts, changing your actions, and reconnecting with your body. You must find and connect with that core sense of who you are. Somewhere deep within you is a knowledge of who you truly are.

Connecting with that part of you can be challenging, but the number one step is reframing your thoughts to recognize your worth. The narcissist has distorted your perception of yourself and the world. However, you can reverse this by changing how you think. In doing this, you can slowly undo your negative beliefs.

It is crucial to actively challenge the negative thoughts and beliefs fueling your feelings of self-doubt, guilt, and shame and then replace them with more positive, realistic thoughts. This shift in mindset is fundamental to rebuilding your sense of self.

How can you start reframing your thoughts?

First, become aware of your negative thought patterns. When you catch yourself thinking something negative, pause and question it. Ask yourself if it's truly accurate or if it's a result of the abuse. Then, replace that negative thought with a positive or neutral one. For example, if you think, "I'm not good enough," counter it with, "I am worthy and capable."

Reframing your thoughts will take time and effort, but it will be worth it. Once you change your thoughts, how you feel about yourself also changes. It makes acknowledging your intrinsic worth possible. You start seeing that, despite what the narcissist would have you believe, their actions weren't a reflection of your value. This realization helps you build a foundation of self-respect, which is essential for healing and moving forward.

Worksheet

This worksheet is designed to help you reframe negative thoughts and beliefs about yourself, replacing them with more positive ones, to gradually reclaim your sense of self.

Step 1: Identify Negative Thoughts

First, identify your recurring negative thoughts. Take a pen and jot down any negative beliefs you hold about yourself. Here's how you can identify them:

1. **Notice Emotional Triggers:**

➤ When do you feel upset, anxious, or down?
➤ What situations or interactions make you feel this way?

2. **Listen to Your Self-Talk:**

➤ What do you say to yourself in challenging moments?
➤ Pay attention to your inner dialogue when you make a mistake or face criticism.

3. **Observe Physical Reactions:**

➤ Notice any physical sensations like a tight chest, stomach knots, or headaches.
➤ These can be signals of underlying negative thoughts.

4. **Write It Down:**

➤ Keep a journal and jot down moments when you feel negative emotions.
➤ Describe what happened, how you felt, and what thoughts crossed your mind.

Examples of common negative thoughts include:

- "I'm not good enough."
- "I don't deserve happiness."

- "I'm always at fault."

Step 2: Challenge Those Thoughts

Now, let's challenge these negative beliefs. For each thought, ask yourself the following questions and write down your responses:

1. **Is this thought based on facts or feelings?**

➤ Are you basing this belief on concrete evidence or how do you feel now? Feelings are valid, but past experiences can influence them and may not always reflect reality.

2. **What's the evidence for and against this belief?**

➤ List out the evidence that supports this thought. Then, write down evidence that contradicts it. This helps you see both sides and can weaken the hold of negative beliefs.

Supporting Evidence: "My last partner constantly criticized me."

Contradicting Evidence: "I have friends and family who love and support me."

3. **Would I say this to a friend in a similar situation?**

➤ Imagine a close friend is going through what you are. Would you tell them they are not good enough or that they don't deserve happiness? Likely not. Treat yourself with the same kindness and compassion.

4. **What are the origins of this belief?**

➤ Consider where this thought comes from. Is it something you heard repeatedly from the narcissist or other negative influences in your life? Recognizing the source can help you understand that it's not an inherent truth about you.

5. **How does this thought affect my life?**

➤ Reflect on how this belief impacts your emotions, behavior, and overall well-being. Understanding the negative consequences can motivate you to change it.

6. **Is there a different way to look at this situation?**

➢ Try to find a different perspective. For instance, instead of thinking, "I'm not good enough," consider, "I'm doing my best and improving every day."

Write down your responses. This step is all about questioning the validity of these thoughts.

Step 3: Reframe Your Thoughts

It's time to reframe!

1. **Consider alternative, more balanced explanations for the thought.**

➢ **Example**: Instead of "I am not deserving of love," think, "My abuser made me feel unlovable, but others value and care about me."

2. **Turn the negative thought into a more positive or neutral one.** Use evidence from the previous step to create a balanced perspective.

➢ **Example**: Reframe "I am not deserving of love" to "I am deserving of love and respect, and I am capable of finding a healthy relationship."

Here's a template to help:

- Negative Thought: _____
- Evidence For: _____
- Evidence Against: _____
- Alternative Explanation: _____
- Reframed Thought: _____

Write down the positive or neutral reframed versions next to the negative ones.

As you work on reclaiming your identity, learn to be kind to yourself. When negative thoughts creep back in, gently remind yourself of the truths you've discovered through this exercise.

Reframing negative thoughts and beliefs about your identity is a process, but you'll see positive changes with practice and persistence. Keep this worksheet handy and revisit it whenever you need a boost.

Congrats on finishing the first part of this book, which was an essential introduction that taught you the core of what to know about narcissists and narcissism. Now that you understand the narcissist as well as anyone can, it's time to delve into the second and third parts, where we will explore the 7 proven strategies for freeing yourself from narcissistic influence.

Keep reading!

PART 2:
The 7 Proven Strategies for Freedom

Life after narcissistic abuse can vary from person to person. Most people believe everything will immediately revert to normal after narcissistic abuse. Nothing is further from reality. Sure, things may improve compared to when you were with the narcissist. However, this period may be even more challenging than the relationship itself. From recovering from the physical and psychological effects to rebuilding an entirely different life, recovering from a narcissistic relationship is a long process that is best started now rather than later.

After deciding to get rid of the narcissist in your life, you may have to start your life from scratch. The scars of the relationship are usually so deep that you have to slowly overcome them step by step. Like many survivors, you may contend with an intense feeling of shame due to many factors.

You may feel shame for letting the narcissist mistreat and demean you how they did. You may feel shame for allowing your kids or pets to be affected by their actions. You may feel shame for not leaving soon. You may even feel shame for finally leaving.

It may be difficult to stop thinking about your ex. You may fixate on the seemingly harmless comments they used to gradually deconstruct your self-worth and self-esteem. You may also think about the fleeting moments when they had nice things to say about you and the good times you had together. Trust me, you will think about everything and even consider returning to them.

This is where the seven proven strategies come into play. These strategies will help you move beyond the abuse to start living your best life again.

It is not enough to survive after narcissistic abuse. You must THRIVE. Let's say someone you know was in a car accident. You don't expect them to stay at the accident site. Once the worst passes and the immediate danger is eliminated, you'd want them to return to their life and work. Even if their future is unknown and unstable after the traumatic experience, you'd expect this person to return home and find the strength to move on with their life.

This is what the seven strategies we're about to explore will help you achieve – thrive instead of just surviving. When you move from victim to survivor who's thriving, that's when you would have reclaimed your life.

By the end of this book, when I have shared all seven strategies, I trust that you will have everything necessary to move on to healthier, happier relationships free of narcissistic influence.

Let's get into it.

CHAPTER FOUR:
Know Your Limits: Defining And Enforcing Healthy Boundaries

When the word "boundaries" is mentioned, what do you think of it? Do you imagine fences that separate you from everyone else? If you do, you may be right…in a sense. However, contrary to what many think, erecting these fences isn't bad. You need them to have healthy, functional relationships with others. Imagine if there wasn't a fence between you and your neighbor's house. How often would you impose on each other's territories?

Boundaries define appropriate and inappropriate behaviors in interpersonal relationships. A simple definition of a boundary is "a limit that defines you as separate from others." Basically, boundaries define what you find acceptable or unacceptable. Think of them as personal rules to maintain your physical and emotional well-being.

Consider how you feel when someone stands too close to you – uncomfortable, right? You might describe this as the person invading your personal space. Not wanting people to stand too close to you is a type of boundary setting.

Boundaries give you a sense of agency over your body, feelings, and physical space. Unfortunately, they aren't as obvious as fences. They are more like an invisible "no trespassing" sign.

It's crucial to set and enforce boundaries after narcissistic abuse. Why? Because they will help protect you and reclaim your sense of self. During the relationship, your boundaries were crossed and violated by the narcissist repeatedly. Narcissists have a knack for pushing other people's limits and undermining their needs. This can leave their victims feeling drained and disrespected. Putting boundaries up is a key step in undoing this and other effects of narcissistic abuse.

If you're still wondering why boundaries are so important, here are a few reasons:

1. **Self-Respect**: Setting boundaries is a way to tell people you want and deserve respect. When you establish necessary limits, it's a sign that you value yourself and recognize your needs as important.
2. **Safety**: A sense of safety comes from affirming your limits. They ensure the abuser can't keep manipulating and exploiting you. This can help you feel more secure in interactions with other people.
3. **Control**: It's normal to feel out of control after leaving an abusive relationship. But with boundaries, you reclaim control over your life and decisions. They empower you to say "no" and mean it.
4. **Emotional Health**: Boundaries ensure you don't have to constantly deal with narcissists or other toxic people. This reduces stress and prevents emotional exhaustion.

Every time I have talked to a survivor of abuse, the common theme of our conversations is that they're unsure of how to set and enforce healthy boundaries. Even when survivors have come a long way in the healing process, they still hesitate to set boundaries.

Do I need to set a boundary here, or am I overreacting? How do I know when it's justified and when it isn't?

These are two questions you will contend with as you try to master the art of boundary-setting after narcissistic abuse. And the short answer to both is that you can set boundaries whenever and wherever you feel like it. You don't need explanations or justifications to set a boundary.

If you feel like you may be "overreacting," that's probably the lingering effect of gaslighting. However, you must be confident and assertive to set and enforce healthy boundaries. I'll come back to this in a subsequent section.

Setting boundaries means:

- determining what you are and aren't responsible for in a relationship.
- defining what you are and aren't comfortable with.
- clarifying where you end, and someone else begins.
- communicating who you are, what you value, and what your limits are.

When you do this, you're protecting everything that matters to you.

It goes without saying that you need boundaries between you and the narcissist after separation. At the same time, you must set boundaries with other toxic people in your life. Not everyone deserves access to your space and life.

The question is, how do you start setting boundaries? This process begins with identifying your discomfort in your personal and professional relationships. Ensure these limits are clear and specific.

Identifying Your Limits

To identify your limits, you must be introspective and honestly assess your thoughts, feelings, needs, and experiences. I have made figuring out one's limits easier by devising the simple process below.

1. **Reflect on past experiences.**

Think about your past interactions, not just with the narcissist but with others as well. Focus on those where you felt disrespected, uncomfortable, or hurt. What specific actions or behaviors made you feel this way? Write them down in a notebook. Examples may include invasion of privacy, yelling, or belittling "jokes."

2. **Tune into your emotions.**

Emotions are some of the best indicators of personal boundaries. Pay attention to how you feel in various situations or around certain people. Do you feel angry, anxious, or drained? These emotions are usually signals of a boundary being crossed or violated.

3. Recognize your values.

What matters to you the most in interactions and relationships? Some shared values among humans are respect, kindness, and honesty. Use these values to define what you will and won't tolerate. For instance, if respect matters to you, disrespectful behavior may be unacceptable.

4. Be specific.

Based on introspection, emotions, and values, develop clear and specific limits to set with others. Specificity is crucial – instead of "I want respect," be specific about what respect means to you. For instance, "I won't tolerate being yelled at or insulted."

5. Consider your needs.

You must factor in your physical, emotional, and social needs to set boundaries that resonate. Think about what you need to feel safe and respected in these aspects of your life. Your limits should cover those needs. For example, "I need time alone to recharge, so I won't accept constant interruptions."

Once you know your limits, it's time to communicate them. When informing others, it helps to be firm but respectful. In other words, you must be assertive, not aggressive. You might feel uncomfortable if you aren't used to setting boundaries; it's part of the process.

- **Be clear and specific.** Vague and ambiguous statements are easily misconstrued. Don't say, "I need space," say, "I need 30 minutes of alone time after work to relax."
- **Use "I" statements**: Instead of framing your boundaries in the context of others' behaviors, focus on your needs and feelings. Also, you don't have to explain or justify them.

State them calmly and confidently. Repeat them if necessary. For example, "I feel overwhelmed when you criticize me in front of others. I need you to discuss issues with me privately."

Narcissists and other toxic people will often push back when you set boundaries with them. So, be ready for some resistance. But do not back down. Your boundaries are non-negotiable.

Here are some examples of boundaries:

- **Time Boundaries**: "I can't stay late at work tonight because I need to spend time with my family."
- **Emotional Boundaries**: "I'm not comfortable discussing this topic. Let's talk about something else."
- **Physical Boundaries**: "I don't like being hugged without being asked first."
- **Material Boundaries**: "I can't lend you my car. It's something I'm not comfortable with."

Start small by practicing boundary-setting in low-pressure situations and environments. This will gradually build your confidence, and over time, it will come naturally to you, even in challenging conditions.

Defining Your Non-Negotiables: What You Will Not Compromise On

How often do you compromise on the things that matter most to you? As someone who has been in a relationship with a narcissist, I'm guessing you do that a lot. Whether it's your health or career, that toxic relationship constantly makes you lose sight of what truly matters. Well, no more of that.

Non-negotiables are what you absolutely won't compromise on, no matter what. Why? Because they're central to your beliefs, values, and goals. Your non-negotiables include what you won't tolerate from others and what you won't tolerate from yourself. They are your main deal-breakers.

In life, non-negotiables can encompass your:

- Relationships
- Career goals
- Physical and mental health
- Daily routines

Common non-negotiables include loyalty, honesty, work-life balance, financial freedom, physical fitness, etc. A good way to think of your non-negotiables is as values so important that you refuse to live without them – under any circumstance. Another way to think of them is as guiding principles that help you prioritize your time and energy and make personal decisions.

Take a minute to think about a belief, hobby, or daily habit that you'll hold onto whatever happens to you right now. That is non-negotiable. Some people see themselves as go-with-the-flow types, but everyone has deeply held beliefs and values that they won't compromise on. These are at the core of who we are and subtly influence our decisions and choices.

What is the difference between setting boundaries and defining non-negotiables? They sound like the same thing, but there's a marked difference. Not all boundaries are non-negotiable. Most boundaries have exceptions, such as people you would relax them for. It depends on their relevance to the situation.

One might say non-negotiables are the stricter forms of boundaries. They are final, and you don't relax them for anyone, no matter what. They revolve around complex issues like fidelity, emotional abuse, physical violence, serious health concerns, and substance use.

After leaving a narcissist, some of the non-negotiables to adopt and enforce in your future relationships include:

- **Honesty**: Integrity and honesty should be non-negotiables. Always expect (and demand) the truth from everyone in your life. Only become intimate with those whose actions align with their values.
- **Respect**: Mutual respect breeds trust. Respect and trust are relationship absolutes. Be with people who value and respect you as a person.
- **Emotional support**: Choose people you can trust to be there for you anytime. They should be willing to listen to and support you when you're having a tough time.
- **Shared values**: Go for people who share your beliefs and priorities regarding life goals, lifestyle, spiritual beliefs, etc. If you get a whim that someone is merely pretending to share your values, get rid of them immediately.

Others include:

- Open communication
- Physical intimacy
- equality

Determining the non-negotiables that are unique to you helps distinguish between core values and flexible preferences. Remember that the only scenario worth considering compromising on a non-negotiable is if it will contribute to personal growth or happiness. Even then, you must be careful not to compromise your integrity or core values.

While the concept of identifying your non-negotiables seems straightforward enough, it can be hard to execute. Many people act instinctually and then evaluate whether their actions align with their values and beliefs. Defining your non-negotiables teaches you to put your values and beliefs first and then act from a place of authenticity.

To define your non-negotiables, create a ranked list of everything that matters to you in life. These may include honesty, learning new things, exploring the world, helping people, living purposefully, or practicing spirituality. List your core values in order.

Using your list of values, develop a top 10 list of things you want to prioritize. Your priorities should tie to your core values. For example, if exploring the world is a core value, a top priority might be visiting 20 or more countries before a specific age.

Next, think about past experiences. What behaviors or situations were deal-breakers for you? It could be dishonesty or lack of communication. Use these insights to add to your list.

Then, consider your goals. Where do you see yourself in the future? What kind of person do you want to be with, or what environment do you want to live in? Your non-negotiables should align with these goals.

Finally, communicate these non-negotiables. Whether with a partner, friends, or even at work, letting others know your boundaries helps avoid misunderstandings and fosters respect.

Remember, defining your non-negotiables means setting standards that protect your peace and ensure your relationships and life choices are healthy and fulfilling as you move on from your past relationship.

Saying No without Guilt: How to Assert Your Boundaries Effectively

No.

One simple word, yet often the hardest to utter. Why do we find it so hard to tell people no sometimes?

For many, the word "no" is typically accompanied by strong feelings of guilt. You may be afraid to disappoint. Or anxious to turn people down. Or you may be a people pleaser.

Growing up with a narcissistic parent or dating a narcissist can make it incredibly challenging to say "no."

As a child or partner, you might find yourself constantly trying to keep the peace and avoid conflict with a narcissist. This can lead to a habit of putting their needs before yours – at the expense of your well-being.

Additionally, you might fear the consequences of saying "no." Narcissists can react with anger, passive-aggressiveness, or even emotional withdrawal. It might seem easier to go along with their demands.

Even if your parents weren't narcissists, the inability to say no can still stem from childhood. As a child, telling adults no is considered a form of backtalk and frowned upon. Sometimes, saying no is met with negative feedback or punishment.

But here's the thing: recognizing this pattern is the first step toward change. It's important to start valuing your own needs and practicing self-assertion. Learning to say "no" will improve your life.

If you have difficulty telling people "NO," you can take the first step by identifying signs of discomfort. This will show you when to draw the line in an interaction. The following signs indicate when it's time to say no:

1. Feeling uncomfortable
2. Feeling obligated or guilty
3. Feeling overwhelmed or overloaded
4. Getting asked to do something that violates a personal boundary
5. Saying yes for no other reason than to please the other person

Mastering the ability to say "no" assertively without feeling guilty begins with recognizing that you're entitled to say no. You're the only one who should dictate how you spend your time and energy. You don't owe the narcissist or anyone else an explanation for wanting to protect your valuable resources. Remember a few things when you start honing this crucial skill.

First, you must start small. Practice saying no in low-stakes situations to build your confidence. For instance, if a friend asks you to go out when you need a night in, say, "Thanks for the invite, but I need some time to myself tonight."

Second, when you say no, be clear and direct. Avoid overly apologizing or giving long explanations. A simple "No, I can't do that," is often enough. You can soften it slightly without diluting your message by saying, "I appreciate the offer, but I can't."

Know your limits and make them known. If someone asks for a favor you're uncomfortable with, say, "I'm not able to help with that." If they push, remain firm. "I understand you need help, but I can't provide that right now."

You may initially feel guilty, especially as you're used to prioritizing others. But always remember that saying no doesn't make you wicked. It's a form of self-care. Think about how you've stretched yourself too thin in your past relationship and the aftermath. Let it serve as a reminder of why putting yourself first is best.

Different Ways to Say No

Having a variety of ways to say no can be helpful. Here are different ways to say no depending on the context and how firm you need to be:

Simple and Direct

1. "No, thank you."
2. "No, I can't."
3. "No, I'm not interested."

Polite but Firm

1. "Thanks for thinking of me, but I have to decline."
2. "I appreciate the offer, but I can't commit to that."

3. "I'm honored, but I can't."

Providing a Reason (Optional)

1. "I wish I could, but I have other commitments."
2. "I'm sorry, but my schedule is full."
3. "I'd love to help, but I need to focus on my priorities right now."

Suggesting an Alternative

1. "I can't, but maybe [name] can help you."
2. "Not right now, but let's find another time."
3. "I'm not available, but how about we reschedule?"

Setting Boundaries

1. "I'm not comfortable with that."
2. "That's not something I can help with."
3. "I need to say no for my own well-being."

Redirecting

1. "This isn't a good time, but thank you for asking."
2. "Let me check my schedule and get back to you."
3. "I'll have to pass this time."

When You've Already Said No

1. "As I mentioned before, I can't do that."
2. "We've already discussed this, and my answer is no."
3. "I've already explained my reasons, and my decision stands."

Using these different ways to say no can help you feel more comfortable and confident in setting boundaries. Choose the one that feels right for you and the situation.

Gray Rocking and Minimal Contact: De-escalate Tension through Limited Engagement

What would you say if I asked you to describe a gray rock in two words? Something like "gray" and "rock," maybe. That's how forgettable and unremarkable gray rocks are. Even enthusiastic rock collectors don't say much about them. There are countless numbers of gray rocks scattered everywhere around you.

What does this mean for you?

It means becoming a gray rock might be your key to escaping notice from the narcissist after you leave them. This is especially true if something still connects you to them, like kids or pets. Of course, you can't turn into a rock. But the good news is that gray rocking can make this happen...figuratively.

Gray Rocking is a technique for limiting interactions with abusive or manipulative people. These can be narcissists or other toxic people without a personality disorder. This technique involves transforming yourself into the most boring, uninteresting person to ever live when interacting with a narcissist.

Narcissists feed on drama and chaos, so the more uninteresting you seem, the more their efforts to stir up drama with you fail.

Recognizing that there's a narcissist in your life may prompt you to start working on leaving them and cutting off contact. Unfortunately, this isn't always 100% achievable. For instance, you might have to meet them at family events, co-parent, or work together.

That's where gray rocking can be super helpful. By transforming into a metaphorical gray rock, you can avoid giving the narcissist any info they might use to undermine you. Eventually, they may stop trying and leave you alone.

This strategy is also great for when you break up or turn down a date with a potentially dysfunctional person, and they don't get the message.

Be Vague – Offer Nothing

When you meet, and the narcissist asks questions you can't avoid, maintain a blank look on your face and give them a vague response. Try an "mm-hmm" or "uh-huh" instead of saying yes or no. Other options include a shrug and an "eh" without eye contact.

Non-committal responses make it seem like you have nothing interesting to offer them. More importantly, they help you avoid the thrill, conflict, and chaos narcissists bring with them everywhere.

Disengage and Detach

Eye contact is a powerful tool for facilitating an emotional connection. Therefore, do not, under any circumstance, maintain eye contact with the narcissist or anyone else you use this strategy for. It's much better to focus on something else or look somewhere else. This will help you remain detached from the interaction.

Disengaging and detaching ensures the narcissist doesn't get the attention they so desperately want from you. It also helps distract you from all manipulation attempts. Even if they make a cruel remark to get a rise out of you, it's less likely to be upsetting if you're disconnected from the conversation. If you get upset, focusing on something else helps prevent a show of emotion.

Keep Interactions Brief

Depending on the nature of your relationship, you may have to engage in fairly regular interactions with the narcissist after separating. For example, if it's your parent or an ex whom you have to co-parent with.

Electronic communication can make a difference here. Talking through the phone helps prevent prolonged conversations that trigger stress and make it harder to be a gray rock. Still, gray rocking works well in all forms of communication.

Just remember to stick to brief and short responses, such as "yes," "no," and "I don't know." Do not explain further. If you're co-parents, limit your interactions to pick-up and drop-off times.

For gray rocking to work effectively, you mustn't tell the narcissist what you're doing. Otherwise, they will find a way to subvert it. The goal is to make them lose interest in interacting with you independently.

Next, let's talk about how you can start healing your wounded inner child.

CHAPTER FIVE:
Healing The Inner Wound: Self-Compassion And Recovery

If there's one thing narcissistic abuse does, it's that it leaves a gaping wound inside victims. This wound results from being discarded, devaluated, and belittled by someone you genuinely care about. It's an invisible wound but can cause great harm if left unattended.

This inner wound is one of abandonment. Being in a relationship where you gave your all and received nothing in return can deeply cut the heart. You may feel empty and invisible, especially because no one else sees that wound.

Being in a relationship where it never felt like you mattered creates an existential wound. It makes you think that you have no place in the world. From research, we know that one of the most potent ways of injuring others emotionally is to remove them from substantial human contact – especially communication.

A common form of abuse by narcissists involves controlling communication in their relationships. This can range from stonewalling to ignoring, not addressing an issue, crazy-making interactions, and unwillingness to resolve a conflict.

One of the narcissist's preferred tactics is the silent treatment. It inflicts deep abandonment wounds on victims. Some are so hurt by it that they turn to medication, substance abuse, or even suicide. All of this is to escape the emptiness that comes from being emotionally neglected.

People cope differently. Some pretend they don't care; some doubt their worth; others become angry and resentful. Your inner wound comes with defense mechanisms.

To heal from this wound, the main solution is to grieve. Though the narcissist wasn't right for you, it's still normal to feel a sense of loss. Grief is the key to healing from loss and emotional hurt.

Here's what you can do to process your grief:

- **Write a letter to the narcissist**. Tell them about everything you're feeling – hurt, anger, confusion, sadness, rejection, etc. Let out your grief. Let them know how they hurt you. You mustn't give this letter to the narcissist, though. The purpose is to help you identify and process your feelings.
- **Explore your feelings of longing**. It's OK if you miss and long for the narcissist. But instead of focusing on the narcissist, explore those feelings instead. Find where the hurt and aches are stored in your body. You can write another letter about the feelings or draw a picture to represent your longing. The goal is to identify how you're experiencing these feelings of longing from a creative perspective.
- **Give in to the feelings**. It's important to let yourself feel. Don't suppress or repress the feelings. The more you give in to them, the quicker you will heal from that inner wound.

In the end, no matter who hurt you, no matter how wounded you are, you still have to thrive. You can still live, hope, love, and be happy. The key is to honor your emotions, acknowledge the loss, and validate the consequences of what you lost.

As you do this, you must simultaneously work on releasing your self-blame. Most survivors struggle with this, so let me show you how to do it.

Releasing Self-Blame: Understand You Were Not the Problem

Guilt, shame, and self-blame are some of the prominent feelings survivors struggle with during the healing and recovery process. Self-blame occurs when you transfer accountability from your abuser to yourself. Throughout the relationship, they made you feel responsible for everything that went wrong. So, you internalize that blame.

Self-blame constitutes a harmful type of emotional abuse. It amplifies your perceived inadequacies and makes moving forward on your healing journey difficult.

If you're a religious person, then you know about the concept of loving-kindness in faith-based religions like Islam, Christianity, and Judaism. This concept also extends to spiritual and para-spiritual communities.

These faith traditions tell us to be kind and loving toward others, and we follow that. But we rarely ever extend that loving-kindness to ourselves. And that's why we deal with a lot of self-blame, especially after abuse.

It's easy to fall into a pattern of constantly blaming yourself for falling for the narcissist, staying in the relationship, leaving the narcissist, missing them, etc. But no matter what you think you were or weren't responsible for, you are never the one at fault for the abuse.

Releasing any form of self-blame is a crucial step in the healing process. If you grew up with a parent who had narcissistic traits, then you must release the self-blame you feel toward both your inner child and your adult self.

Your abuser is the only one who should ever feel guilty and ashamed for their actions. It wasn't your responsibility. You weren't at fault. You are not the one to blame. Therefore, there's no reason to accept the guilt or shame.

The reality is that releasing self-blame isn't as easy as it sounds. People who lack empathy cannot feel shame. As such, anyone who experiences shame is also capable of managing it. In the words of a wise person, "Empathy is the antidote to shame."

With this in mind, some steps you can take to release your self-blame include:

- Being empathetic toward yourself.
- Write about how you feel in a journal. Write about the shame, guilt, and self-blame you feel. Then, stare at it. Doing this lessens the power of these feelings over you.
- Talking to someone you trust about it.
- Address the self-blame in a letter. For example, you might write a letter to the "you" who experienced the abuse and explain that it wasn't your fault – you aren't to blame.
- When you feel blame and shame creeping up, recite this mantra: "What I did or didn't do doesn't matter. I am not to blame for how my abuser treated me."

Through the process of releasing the toxic emotion of self-blame, you will become aware of every negative thing you internalized from the narcissist. Then, you can redistribute these feelings that aren't yours to the rightful owner: the narcissist who abused you.

In doing this, you will regain control of your reality and move forward in this journey.

Practicing Forgiveness (of Yourself): Let Go of Anger and Resentment

Anger and resentment are major obstacles to overcoming narcissistic abuse. It's no news that both emotions are unhealthy for the mind and body. Even years after getting rid of the narcissist, you can "move on" while still storing anger and resentment in your body. This often manifests through anxiety, irritability, depression, substance use, addiction, and mood problems. So, it's clear why you must let go of any anger and resentment you feel and embrace forgiveness – not just of the narcissist, but of yourself as well.

Narcissistic abuse understandably causes a lot of anger in victims, especially because of the abuser's lack of remorse. The narcissist will not acknowledge, accept, or apologize for how they treated you. They might brag about what they did. This isn't helpful. It's hard not to be angry and resentful when your abuser is so obnoxious or unrepentant about their actions. But these emotions will only impede your healing progress.

Forgiveness is the only way to deliberately let go of anger and resentment toward the person who wronged you. But while it's always so easy to forgive others, you may have difficulty embracing self-forgiveness.

Everyone has bad experiences. We all make mistakes. However, learning to let go, forgive yourself, and move forward benefits your emotional and mental well-being.

Now, you might be thinking forgiveness entails pretending the abuse wasn't real or that it wasn't "that serious." This isn't the case. Practicing forgiveness toward yourself and your abuser is about:

- Understanding your emotions
- Accepting the role you played in what happened
- Treating yourself kindly and compassionately
- Making amends to yourself
- Finding lessons from the experience
- Focusing on how to make better choices in the future

Forgiveness means accepting what has happened and being willing to move past it without fixating on something you can't change.

Once you acknowledge that you're angry and resentful, you must accept that you will feel lighter and happier without these feelings. They are burdens. So, you must let go.

First, here's a simple exercise to help you start freeing yourself from the burden of anger and resentment.

1. **Find a Quiet Space**: Sit comfortably and close your eyes.

2. **Practice Deep Breathing**: Breathe deeply and exhale slowly. Do this several times to relax.
3. **Visualize the Person**: Picture the person who hurt you. This can be tough, but it's crucial.
4. **Acknowledge Your Feelings**: Allow yourself to feel the anger and pain. **Don't push it away.**

- **Speak** Your Forgiveness: Silently or out loud, say, "I forgive you for what you did. I release the hold this anger has over me."
- **Let Go**: Visualize the anger and resentment leaving your body. Imagine it dissolving into the air.
- **Focus on Peace**: Picture yourself feeling calm and free from the weight of these emotions.

Repeat this exercise as needed. Forgiveness is a process, not a one-time event.

Now, here's another exercise to practice forgiving yourself each day.

1. **Find a Quiet Space**. Opt for a serene location where interruptions are unlikely. This is your time to focus on yourself.
2. **Set the Mood**. Light a candle, play soft music, or diffuse essential oils to create a calming atmosphere.
3. **Take Deep Breaths**. Sit comfortably and close your eyes. Take a series of deep breaths, breathing in through your nose and out through your mouth. Allow your body to relax with each breath.
4. **Reflect on Your Emotions**. Think about the anger and resentment you're holding onto. Acknowledge these feelings without judgment. It's OK to feel this way.

5. **Visualize the Release**. Picture yourself holding onto a heavy object that represents your anger and resentment. Imagine how it feels in your hands.
6. **Affirm Your Forgiveness**. Silently or out loud, say, "I forgive myself for holding onto this anger and resentment. I am human, and I am learning. I choose to let go of these feelings."
7. **Let Go**. Visualize yourself gently placing the heavy object down or releasing it into the air. Watch it disappear, feeling the weight lift from your shoulders.
8. **Embrace Self-Compassion**. Place your hand over your heart and repeat these affirmations: "I am worthy of forgiveness. I am deserving of peace. I am letting go of what no longer serves me."

Practice this exercise daily. Forgiveness is a journey, and it's OK to take your time. Be patient and gentle with yourself. You're doing important work; every step forward gets you closer to finishing.

Nourishing Your Soul: Strategies for Emotional and Physical Recovery

As you continue your journey of healing, you are likely to still deal with the aftermath of narcissistic abuse. It will take significant time for the psychological and physical effects to go away completely. In some cases, they may not, but they will be reduced to an insignificant level. Whether it's anxiety, depression, dissociation, flashbacks, or physical illness, you will need self-care to nourish your soul and keep yourself feeling good.

Ongoing self-care practices are backed by research as being powerful in helping victims or survivors of narcissistic abuse heal more quickly. They are great for tending to your mind, body, and spirit.

Though these healing modalities may not work the same for everyone, exploring and finding one that meets your needs will be exceedingly beneficial in the long term.

The following three self-care strategies will aid your emotional and physical recovery on this incredible journey.

1. Meditation

Narcissistic abuse can be traumatizing. Experiencing trauma can disrupt the areas of your brain responsible for executive functions like learning, planning, memory, focus, and self-regulation. They, essentially, become disrupted.

Science has shown that meditation can benefit the same areas disrupted by trauma, including the prefrontal cortex, amygdala, and hippocampus. Meditating strengthens the neural pathways in those areas, increases grey matter density, and regulates your instinctual reaction to the "fight or flight" activation.

You also become more aware of your emotions and cravings, which helps ensure you don't react impulsively to triggers. For example, it can stop you from breaking No Contact with the narcissist and impede your progress.

2. Yoga

Trauma is stored in the body. That's why an activity like Yoga, which combines physicality and mindfulness, can help restore mind-body balance. Research has shown that Yoga can help ease stress, anxiety, and depression. It can also strengthen resilience and self-regulation and improve self-esteem.

The science is that Yoga allows you to attain self-mastery. This helps to regain ownership over your body. You're able to cultivate a sense of feeling safe within your body. It can also help with dissociation by teaching you to tune into your bodily sensations.

3. Positive Affirmations

Part of healing is reprogramming your brain to let go of the negative messages you've internalized from the narcissist. Positive affirmations can make this happen for you. It helps to develop a system of positive affirmations tailored to your inner wounds and insecurities.

Let's say your abuser has made you insecure about your body. In that case, you can use positive affirmations to counter the pattern of negative thinking in that area. The key is to repeat a simple and loving thought, such as "I am beautiful, within and out," whenever you get that toxic thought or the associated emotions.

The best way to use affirmations is to say them out loud, perhaps in front of a mirror. Another way is to record different affirmations in your voice and listen to them each day, mornings, and evenings.

Examples include:

- "I am worthy and deserving of love."
- "I am valuable."
- "I love myself."
- "I am beautiful."
- "My body is a work of art."

It's a great method for rewriting the ugly narratives the narcissists planted in your head. Self-care is paramount, so we will explore how to implement self-care into your daily routine.

For now, the next chapter is all about reclaiming your voice and identity. Get ready to learn how to reframe the narratives the narcissist fed you about yourself!

CHAPTER SIX:
Reframing Your Narrative: Reclaiming Your Voice

Narratives are powerful. They shape our perception of ourselves and everything else around us. If someone tells you repeatedly that you aren't worthy of love, that narrative can stick. When you've been in a relationship with a narcissist, that is exactly what happens. Controlling the narrative is one of the most powerful tools narcissists use against their victims. Unfortunately, their narratives often stick. This is where narrative therapy comes in.

Imagine you own a book. This book is filled with many chapters. Each chapter contains a story that others – like the narcissist – have written about you. None of the stories are good, though. They don't make you feel good about yourself. They evoke many negative emotions. But you're stuck with carrying this book around for life.

Narrative therapy can help you rewrite that book and change the stories. In other words, it's an approach that enables you to rewrite the narrative about your abuse. This approach centers the narcissist, not you, as the problem and the villain. It helps you detach yourself from their actions and the issues they have caused.

Here's one way to look at it: Instead of saying, "I am a victim," narrative therapy teaches you to change that to "Someone's harmful behavior has hurt me." This language shift may seem trivial, but it's powerful enough to change how you see yourself going forward. Rewriting the narrative is all about embracing your power as the sole author of your story and using that power for good.

Reclaiming your voice involves two steps: externalizing the issue and rewriting the narrative. These two steps are all you need to take back control of your life and story after narcissistic abuse.

1. **Externalizing the Issue**

First, you must extract the problem from within you and create its own space. This begins with recognizing that the traumatic experience didn't reflect who you are. Yes, it happened to you. No, it's not your identity. Externalizing allows you to assess the issue objectively instead of addressing it as an innate part of your identity.

Once you put the problem in its place, the next step is reframing your narrative.

2. **Rewriting Your Narrative**

What have you been telling yourself and others about the abuse? It's time to pick up a pen and examine the truth of it. Are these stories factual, or are they fiction created by the narcissist? Then, start reframing them individually – telling stories that reflect your worth, strength, and resilience.

Rewriting your narrative is about more than changing how you talk about yourself. It's also about changing how you see yourself. It's about realizing that the power to define yourself lies with you. Don't let what you experienced define you.

Think of this step as replacing the lens through which you view your past. Instead of looking at yourself through the narcissist's distorted lens, start seeing yourself in a new light. Challenge the old narratives with evidence of your true self.

Finally, you must embrace a new narrative. This involves accepting the past and committing to moving forward with the new narrative. In this, you become a resilient survivor, not a victim.

Of course, you need practical tips to engage in narrative therapy on your own. A powerful tip is re-telling your life story. You reframe every major thing that has happened to you to highlight your strengths and resilience. Another is looking for alternative stories where you demonstrated courage and compassion. These stories should be a stark contrast to the narratives the narcissist fed you.

Use these tips to actively rewrite your narrative about the abuse. In doing so, you can find yourself and reclaim your identity. This will help you stay on the path toward total recovery.

Journaling for Insight: Processing Your Experience and Gaining Clarity

A journal is the most therapeutic thing you can own as a survivor of a dysfunctional dynamic. Believe me when I say journaling is a remarkably powerful tool. Sadly, people don't often realize this until they try it. Healing requires you to reflect and feel. It's impossible to heal and recover without feeling your way through the pain. There is no way around it. Journaling helps you think.

Maintaining a journal to record your feelings and experiences is a habit that everyone should cultivate. Often, people who have survived narcissistic abuse spend years looking for their hero in others. But the truth is that you're the only hero who could ever have the biggest impact on yourself.

What exactly makes journaling so great?

Journaling helps you process emotions, vent safely, and regain your sense of self. Writing about your experiences can rebuild your identity and track your progress, showing how far you've come. Plus, it breaks negative thought cycles, which instills a much more positive mindset.

So, here are some journaling prompts for you to start processing your feelings:

1. **How am I feeling right now?**
   - Take a moment to check in with yourself. Are you happy, sad, anxious, or excited? Write it all down.
2. **What has been on my mind lately?**

- Reflect on the thoughts that have been occupying your mind. Is there something specific that's been bothering you or making you happy?
3. **What am I grateful for today?**
- Focusing on gratitude can shift your perspective. List at least three things you're thankful for right now.
4. **What do I need to let go of?**
- Recognize any negative thoughts or emotions that are burdening you. What can you release to feel lighter?
5. **What are three things I did well today?**
- Reflect on your accomplishments, no matter how small.
6. **How did I feel during a specific interaction today?**
- Describe an interaction and how it made you feel. What does this tell you about your boundaries?
7. **What is one step I can take to feel more in control?**
- Identify a small, actionable step to regain control over your life.
8. **Who in my life makes me feel safe, and why?**
- List the people who provide emotional safety. How can you spend more time with them?
9. **How can I practice self-compassion today?**
- Think of a specific way to be kind to yourself. What words or actions will support you?
10. **What activities help me feel calm and centered?**
- List activities that reduce anxiety and promote peace. Plan to incorporate them into your routine.
11. **What positive affirmations can I repeat to myself?**
- Create affirmations that boost your self-esteem. How can you integrate them into your daily life?
12. **How do I feel about my progress so far?**
- Reflect on your healing journey. What progress have you made, and how can you continue to grow?
13. **What boundaries do I need to set to protect myself?**

- Identify specific boundaries that will help you feel safe. How can you communicate these?

14. How can I nurture my inner child today?
- Think of an activity that brings joy to your inner child. How can you include it in your day?

15. What qualities do I admire in myself?
- List qualities you appreciate about yourself. How can you remind yourself of these traits?

The answers to your recovery lie within you, and these journaling prompts will help you connect with them.

Sharing Your Story: Find Comfort and Validation through Support Groups

It's normal for survivors of narcissistic abuse to feel like no one understands what they've been through. This is a feeling you will experience constantly as you work on healing. Sharing your story is a powerful step to address and overcome that feeling, and support groups provide the perfect environment to do just that.

A support group targeted specifically at survivors of narcissistic abuse isn't just a great avenue to share your story. It's also a safe space to receive all the validation, empathy, and emotional support you need. Even better, these things come from people who know exactly what you've been through. At the same time, a support group can be a great place to get information to help you understand your experience on a deeper and more personal level.

Social support is a huge component of healing and recovery. It makes sense when you consider that narcissists isolate their victims from everyone else. Needing support to heal isn't a bad thing. You need to know and feel that you aren't alone. You need all the support you can get, and the best kind is from people who understand what it's like to be in your shoes.

In a narcissistic abuse recovery support group, survivors can come together and help each other heal through the abuse by providing validation. It is a space where you can expect to be listened to, heard, validated, and supported by other survivors. Hearing others who have had that experience share what they overcame can help you realize that healing is achievable. These people won't judge, dismiss, or invalidate your experience or feelings. It's a great addition to therapy or any other approach you take. You should make it a core part of your journey.

Here's what a support group will do for you:

- **Feel less isolated**. Realizing you're not alone can be incredibly comforting. Hearing others share their stories reminds you that your experiences are valid.
- **Gain new perspectives.** Listening to how others have coped and healed can offer new insights and strategies for your recovery.
- **Build resilience**. Support groups can strengthen your ability to face challenges and rebuild your life with the encouragement and support of others.

Let me tell you what happens in a support group. Usually, members meet regularly online or in person. They take turns sharing their experiences, offering insights and advice, and providing emotional support to each other. You must decide how much you want to share with your group based on comfort.

Keep in mind that it's a judgment-free zone. You're all there to support one another; each person's story is valuable. As you find comfort, you must also offer understanding and hope to others.

The question now is, how do you find the right support group for you?

You can begin by looking for a mental health provider in your local area. Ask them to refer you to any narcissistic abuse support group near you. They should be able to share valuable information or steer you in the right direction. Another option is to check online for support groups to join.

Some resources that can help in that regard include:

- **Psychology Today**: Their online directory can help you find support groups led by licensed therapists in your area.
- **Narcissist Abuse Support (dot com):** This website offers resources and directories for support groups specifically for survivors of narcissistic abuse.
- **Meetup**: Search for local groups focused on healing from narcissistic abuse or emotional abuse.
- **The Mighty**: An online community that offers support and resources for people dealing with various health challenges, including emotional and narcissistic abuse.
- **Support Groups Central**: Offers a variety of online support groups, including those focused on emotional and narcissistic abuse.

Remember, don't just go to a random support group. It's best to join a space specifically for people like you. Many organizations and therapists offer these groups, both locally and online. Don't be afraid to try a few different ones to see which fits best.

The mere thought of sharing your story with strangers can be frightening, but this step is worth taking. Support groups provide a unique environment where you can find comfort and validation. They remind you that you're not alone and that healing is possible. So, take that first step and find a group today.

Finding Yourself Again: Rediscover Yourself, Strengths, Passions, and Purpose

Look at yourself in the mirror - who do you see? After what you've been through, it might feel like looking at a stranger. Right now, it's quite likely that you don't know who you are. That's what narcissistic abuse does to you.

At this very moment, you're on an adventure to find yourself again. If you were a victim of a narcissistic parent-child dynamic, then you've probably never known who you are. This is an opportunity to find the real you and let go of the person you became to please a toxic mother or father.

Many survivors have difficulty finding themselves after abuse. Some even lose themselves more along the way. They learn that they should have taken a left when they took a right turn. Rediscovering your passions, strengths, and purpose to find your whole self comes with challenges. However, it's part of the process.

You will need a jump-off point to discover everything that will make you who you want to be going forward. Direction and a better understanding of how to achieve self-discovery are crucial.

Finding yourself means realizing who you truly are as an individual. This is unique to each person, but ultimately, it's about what we want out of life. In an earlier chapter, we talked about how to reclaim your sense of self after narcissistic abuse.

Here, we will look at practical tips to help you find your authentic self.

Try new activities.

What are things you like doing? Think about your favorite hobbies and activities before the relationship. If nothing comes to mind, experiment with these activities:

- Painting
- Drawing
- Pottery
- Sculpture
- Writing
- Photography

- Learning a musical instrument
- Yoga
- Pilates
- Hiking or nature walks
- Dancing (salsa, ballroom, hip-hop, etc.)
- Rock climbing
- Cycling
- Reading books (fiction, non-fiction, self-help)
- Learning a new language
- Enrolling in online courses (Coursera, Udemy, etc.)
- Joining a book club
- Volunteering at local charities

Remember, the goal is to have as many new experiences as possible to see what connects with you.

Create an interesting journal.

Start a journal dedicated to having new experiences. Write down anything that piques your interest during your day-to-day life. This could be a random activity, an idea, or a topic. Give it time, and you'll start noticing patterns that can point to your unidentified interests.

For this journal to succeed, focus on activities and interests you instinctively gravitate towards. For instance, what movies do you like watching in your free time? What books do you find yourself reading? Your curiosity can direct you toward your passions.

Try mind mapping.

Mind mapping is an excellent visual tool for exploring your interests and passions. Begin with a general concept like "What I love." Create branches from this central idea into categories such as "Skills," "Hobbies," "Experiences," and "Causes." Each represents different things you might be curious about. Now, add more specific and relevant items under each branch. For instance, you might add "painting" under "Hobbies" and "helping animals" under Causes.

Making a mind map helps you organize your thoughts and uncover connections or patterns, making it easier to discover your interests, passions, and strengths.

Do a strengths assessment.

A strengths assessment test, such as CliftonStrengths or VIA Character Strengths Survey can offer valuable insights into your innate talents and abilities. Another way to learn your strengths is to reflect on past accomplishments. How did you make them happen? What skills did you use? Responding to these questions can illuminate your strengths and weaknesses. You can also request feedback from people who know you well. Ask them about your strengths and how they've seen you use them effectively.

Finding yourself again after getting rid of a narcissist will take time. But these strategies will make rediscovering your strengths, interests, and passions much easier.

We have reached the end of part 2. So far, we've covered three of the seven proven strategies. These are the most crucial for your healing. Now, it's time to explore the last four strategies in this book's third and final part. There, we will look at the best strategies to help you build a brand new life and thrive instead of just surviving after narcissistic abuse.

Let's get into it!

PART 3:
Building a New Life: Thriving After Narcissistic Abuse

"Can I build a new life now?"

"Will I be able to live happily ever after?"

"Will I ever love or trust again?"

These and more are questions survivors of narcissistic abuse often have as they continue to navigate healing. You're probably asking them in your head, too.

The answer is YES. You can build a new life. You can learn to trust again. You can fall in love again. You can live happily ever after.

Yes, you can do anything you want if you put your mind to it. Intention is critical to achieving what you want. So, tell yourself you can and want to do all these things again.

My favorite thing about being human is our incredible resilience. It is so powerful that even when we experience trauma or adversity, the mind and body adapt. Most importantly, they heal. Don't take this as just something to give you hope – it's backed by science.

The human brain is capable of change and recovery. It can adapt and rewire itself, a process called neuroplasticity. Trauma can be mitigated and overcome with time and, most importantly, effort.

Breaking free from a narcissist gives a newfound sense of freedom and self-awareness. Once you're no longer in that toxic environment, you will start rediscovering yourself…if you put in the necessary effort.

You get to engage in introspection, learn more about your needs and boundaries, and start taking care of your mind, body, and soul. This process isn't just about recovering from abuse, though. It's also about building a new life and thriving in ways you might not have imagined.

Additionally, extensive and varied support systems help you along the way. Whether it's therapy, support groups, books, or online communities, you have access to a wealth of resources that will help you rebuild your life.

Furthermore, if you successfully get through your healing and recovery phase, you will develop a new set of strengths and skills that will prove invaluable for the rest of your life. Be ready to acquire a heightened sense of empathy, build resilience, and know how to spot red flags and toxicity. These incredible qualities will help you create new, healthier relationships and achieve your personal goals moving forward.

Finally, you have the element of personal growth. Trust me when I say this healing process will result in amazing personal development. Once again, this is if you're willing to do the work required. Slowly, you will discover new hobbies, careers, or relationships that align better with the new you and your desired life.

Your growth won't only heal the wound caused by the abuse. It will help you build a richer and more fulfilling life.

So, yes, you can build a new life and thrive after narcissistic abuse. How do you do this? That's what you'll find out in this final part of How to Get Rid of a Narcissist and the chapters within.

The journey may challenge you, but the potential for growth and happiness surpasses the difficulties. With time and self-compassion, you will move past your trauma and build a new life that's different and much better in ways you can't even begin to imagine.

Now, we'll begin by looking at how you can start rebuilding healthy connections and relationships.

CHAPTER SEVEN:
From Isolation To Connection: Building Healthy Relationships

Humans are social creatures. We are wired for connection. Therefore, our interpersonal relationships constitute a huge part of defining ourselves and finding meaning in life. Healthy relationships are critical for our overall health and well-being. They are rich sources of deep emotional connection and happiness. We need them to live a life of value and joy.

Establishing new connections and relationships after an abusive situation is one of the hardest things you'll ever have to do, if not the hardest. Understandably, having a narcissist in your life may have made you skeptical about humans and interpersonal relationships. Now, you may be unsure how to go from isolation to building new relationships.

The reality is that not all relationships are positive or enriching. As you now know from experience, some of them are toxic and dysfunctional. Naturally, you want to avoid those types as you move forward.

When someone's friend, partner, coworker, or family member, gives silent treatment or makes harmful little remarks about you, that's a sign of toxicity. These are all examples of relationship red flags.

Recognizing red flags in a relationship may sound logical, but it's not as easy. What's a red flag? Think of it as a warning signal that indicates when someone isn't suitable to be in your life.

Relationships, particularly intimate partner ones, have nuances. So, it can be difficult to assess whether a relationship is toxic. This is why many people miss the red flags.

Still, the best way to determine if a new relationship is potentially dysfunctional and toxic is to watch for common red flags. Some red flags are universal, whereas others are unique to us based on our non-negotiables.

Here are some behaviors to watch out for in new relationships:

- Repeat violation of your boundaries and an unwillingness to acknowledge or respect them.
- Consistent disrespectful, condescending, snide, or hurtful comments or interactions.
- An unshakeable feeling of worry, fear, or anxiety about the other person, which is amplified by your interactions.
- Refusing to address or deal with issues.
- Consistently refusing to cater to your wants and needs.
- Controlling behavior, such as monitoring your communication or access to friends and family, and irrational possessive behavior.
- Deliberately neglecting or excluding you from things.
- Deliberately exposing you to harmful situations against your will.
- Emotional manipulation.
- Undermining your choices and decisions.

These red flags can manifest in physical, verbal, financial, and sexual interactions. If you let them persist, they will develop into more serious dysfunctional behaviors.

Now, how do you recognize healthy relationships? Here are some green flags to watch out for:

1. **Communication**: Good communication is critical. You shouldn't hesitate to discuss anything and everything with this new person. If you can't, then you must rethink the relationship. Also, are they open and honest with you? Do they listen to you without interrupting or speaking over you?

2. **Respect**: As the saying goes, respect is reciprocal. Whoever you're building a relationship with should always respect your boundaries, opinions, and individuality. Notice if they appreciate you for yourself or want you to change.
3. **Trust**: Trust forms the cornerstone of a healthy relationship. You should feel secure and confident in the other person's actions. If you find yourself doubting their intentions due to their actual behavior, that's a sign to evaluate the relationship.
4. **Support**: Healthy relationships are characterized by mutual support. Regardless of your relationship type, this person should be your cheerleader. They should encourage you to go after your dreams and goals. More importantly, they should be there for you during difficult times.
5. **Equality**: A healthy relationship is one where both have an equal say. Make decisions together and consider both parties' needs. They should make you feel like you are equals and vice versa.
6. **Independence**: Having your own space, interests, and life is a no-brainer. If they don't let you have a life outside of the relationship, take that as your cue to get rid of them early.

It's important to take small steps as you work on making healthy connections. Take things slowly. Don't rush into new relationships, romantic or otherwise. Pay attention to how they treat you and others over time. You're more aware than you think. If you feel something is off in your gut, listen to it. If things feel too good to be true, they are.

Consistency is also important. Notice if their words align with their actions. Do they treat you well consistently, not just when it's convenient for them? Do they meet your needs? Are you on the same page about what you want from the relationship?

Finally, set and enforce your boundaries. This is the most important tip. This new person should respect your limits. Don't be pressured into doing things you're uncomfortable with.

Building new, healthier relationships will happen gradually. After your experience, it's OK to be cautious and protective. You deserve relationships where you feel valued, respected, and loved and can build them.

Setting Boundaries in New Relationships: Protect Yourself from Future Manipulation

So, you're gradually meeting new people and building new relationships. But you're scared – what if you fall to old patterns? What if you find yourself in the same situation again? Absolutely not!

Toxic and manipulative people are everywhere – your home, school, the workplace, the gym, church, etc. You can find dysfunctional individuals anywhere humans are. It's not just narcissists, though. Even people without NPD or other mental disorders can be quite exploitative and dysfunctional as long as they have specific traits.

There are two primary reasons why others might try to manipulate you:

1. To control a situation or your relationship
2. To evade personal responsibility

That's why it is important to take the necessary steps for protection.

The basic premise of protecting yourself from manipulation is to stop seeking others' approval. This means that you shouldn't let yourself be defined by others.

Manipulation only works if you don't know better and you let it. From everything we've discussed in this book, you know better.

Someone looking to take advantage of you will study and use your limitations against you.

The only way to ensure they don't succeed is to not care about whatever they try to convey to you. See their ploys for what they are – mere attempts at controlling you. Do not wait for them to change. You can't control their actions, but you can kick them out of your life…without a second thought. Let them manipulate if they want; they must take it elsewhere.

To do this, you must set and enforce your boundaries. We already discussed boundary-setting extensively. Still, you could always gain more insight.

Boundaries are necessary in various relationships – from friends and family to coworkers and mere acquaintances. But they are much more essential in intimate partner relationships. When you start toying with dating a new person after your ex, you must get ready to enter the relationship with your boundaries intact.

In a romantic dynamic, three variables are at play: yourself, your partner, and the relationship itself. Each variable must have clearly defined boundaries, and all three must be nourished, sustained, and respected.

Though there are general rules to follow when setting and enforcing boundaries in a new relationship, what works for someone else might not be right for you. For example, you and your new partner may have different expectations of:

- How much time you spend together
- How often do you communicate when apart
- What counts as infidelity in a committed relationship
- Lines that can be crossed in terms of your finances

And as you know, boundaries are flexible. So, these may evolve during your relationships. You will find having numerous conversations about your expectations and guidelines incredibly helpful. This will help establish healthy boundaries that factor in both of your needs.

To do this, you must communicate your expectations openly and honestly. More importantly, you must both honor each other's boundaries to create a relationship where everyone feels safe.

We all have our own space and comfort levels regarding personal boundaries. Setting boundaries in a new relationship is about mutual respect and showing each other, "I love you for who you are, and I will respect the lines that you draw."

Here are examples of boundaries you MUST set when you meet a new partner. The limits also apply to other relationships, with responsibility and expectations for both parties, such as co-parents, in-laws, and business partners.

In your relationship, you must both:

- Take each other's feelings and needs into account
- Ask for permission
- Show gratitude
- Be honest
- Leave space for autonomy and reject codependence
- Be respectful of differences in perspective, feelings, and opinions
- Take responsibility for your actions
- Sit with your communication of emotions and needs

While you should set boundaries, some are unhealthy and can harm one or both parties. Such boundaries are rooted in control, where one partner may try to dictate or restrict the other partner's actions. Watch out for any boundary that limits your options. Whether it's around time, how you act, or how you dress, that's a major red flag.

Do not conflate control for boundaries – they're two different things. If you feel this new person is setting boundaries to control you –

"This is my boundary, and it's what you must adhere to" – that's a problem.

There are different ways to set boundaries in a new relationship. My favorite approaches are to:

1. **Start early**: The best time to communicate your boundaries is in the early phase of a relationship. Do not wait months down the road. At that point, there will be emotional investment, and it may be harder to back out if you spot red flags.
2. **Have awkward conversations**: You can't avoid this. No matter how awkward you feel, it helps to have two-way conversations about your boundaries. Remember that communication is key.
3. **Ask for space**. When you're starting, don't be afraid to ask for some alone time whenever you need it. If they react strongly to that request, that's worth considering. Still, be mindful of their feelings when you take this step.

Setting boundaries should be an expected part of future relationships. So, be ready to determine what they are for yourself, your partner, and the relationship.

Rekindling Old Connections: Reconnect with Supportive People from Your Past

Isolation is a painful reality for victims and survivors of abuse. The narcissist may have deliberately separated you from the people who love and support you. It's a part of their M.O. and a tactic to gain greater power and control over you.

They might have demanded that you spend less time with loved ones or even people they think you're attracted to. They could have asked you to stop hanging out at your favorite places or engaging in activities you enjoy. These are absurd expectations that have no place in normal functioning relationships.

You have every right to be part of a strong social support network and community because you're wired to socialize and connect.

After leaving a toxic dynamic, it's normal to feel lonely and frustrated due to the lack of support caused by isolation. A community of friends, family, associates, neighbors, and community members is fundamental to your healing and recovery journey. These people can provide all kinds of support.

They can be there emotionally, keep important documents, or help you through the "No Contact" process. They can also aid your self-care and provide reassurance during tough times. There are so many things they can do for you.

Rekindling connections and rebuilding your support network after leaving an abusive situation can be scary. It's even more terrifying if "bad blood" brewed between you and members of your support group due to the pressure from your narcissistic abuser.

Based on research, the best thing you can do is to reach out and be vulnerable. That feeling of being emotionally exposed can help you reconnect with others by bringing you closer to them. Reflect on what happened between you and those supportive people, and send them an email, a letter, or a message. Be honest and open about your experience and the desire to have them back in your circle.

You should know that some people may reject you, especially if they don't understand narcissistic abuse. Not many people know what it's like or why it's hard to leave. If you can, make them see why you had to do everything you did while with the narcissist. But I believe the affirmative and supportive responses from your loved ones may genuinely surprise you.

Remember to stay safe as you work on moving from isolation to connecting with new and old friends.

In the next chapter, we'll talk about Post-Traumatic Growth (PTG) and how it can help you chart a new course in life.

CHAPTER EIGHT:
Prioritizing Self-Growth: Embracing Personal Development After Abuse

You're aware of post-traumatic stress disorder (PTSD). It's something we've mentioned in this book a few times, and it's one of the aftermaths of suffering narcissistic abuse. Debilitating anxiety, flashbacks, and disturbing thoughts characterize PTSD. But do you know about post-traumatic growth? Most people don't.

Post-traumatic growth occurs when positive changes occur in a trauma survivor's life that improves their quality of life. Sometimes, trauma can be a catalyst for growth. In the best scenarios, it can lead to growth, resilience, and strength.

When you've experienced narcissistic abuse, it may have hurt so bad that it feels like nothing will ever be the same again. Understandably, people often find it difficult to imagine something good from a traumatic experience. But, as you heal and recover, you might notice that your experience has facilitated good change and growth over time.

Right now, you may not feel that what you experienced has a deeper meaning. Yet, as I told you before, being human means you're inherently capable of adapting to even the toughest situations.

For some, post-traumatic growth equates to a greater appreciation for life or increased personal strength. It could be spiritual growth or evolved belief systems. For others, it means the motivation to help others around them.

Every individual processes trauma differently, and the path toward healing is often long. Subsequently, you may find growth in places where you least expect it.

Post-traumatic growth is part of the natural human capacity to heal, learn, and make meaning from hardship. In the 1990s, Richard Tedeschi and Lawrence Calhoun developed the theory of Post-Traumatic Growth. This theory posits that humans achieve positive growth after a crisis or adversity. This growth could happen in their worldview, relationships, or other personal aspects.

During your recovery process, you will expect to face challenges in different areas of your life. The amount of time this takes will vary from person to person. There's no "right" timeline for healing and recovering from the trauma inflicted by narcissistic abuse.

Eventually, you may start to notice growth that wasn't present before you had that traumatic experience.

Common signs of growth include:

- Appreciating life in a way you didn't before
- Developing a stronger sense of closeness with your loved ones and others
- Increased compassion toward yourself and others
- Developing new interests and passions
- Finding a new path in life
- Willingness to make necessary changes
- Knowing that you're stronger than you thought and can handle challenges
- Increased sense of self-reliance
- Stronger faith or deeper understanding of spirituality

You might notice more meaning or clarity about your experience and a sense of moving forward in life despite it.

Based on the PTG theory, the following are strategies for facilitating post-traumatic growth:

- **Education**: After your experience, you must challenge negative beliefs and assumptions to facilitate growth and personal development. This means rethinking your circumstances. Educating yourself will help you develop new thought processes and learn new coping mechanisms for dealing with the aftermath.
- **Emotional regulation**: You can learn, change, adapt, or grow after narcissistic abuse unless you're in the right mind frame. That means learning to manage the emotions that will arise, such as anger, guilt, shame, etc. You must also put the sense of loss behind you. Exercise, relaxation techniques, and mindfulness practice can help you master regulating your emotions.
- **Disclosure**: This means talking about the abuse and how it's impacted you with others. It's a great way to reflect on your experience and process it.
- **Service**: After the abuse, you can do better by helping others who have had a similar experience or donate to organizations working to ensure others don't find themselves in the same situation. You can also volunteer your time or expertise.

To achieve post-traumatic growth, you must:

1. **Process the trauma**. Open yourself to the depth of your experience. Do not suppress or avoid the accompanying feelings.
2. **Reflect on beliefs**. How has the abuse challenged or reinforced your beliefs? Answer this question to reassess your core values and beliefs and understand what matters.
3. **Seek professional help**. If you can't do it on your own, don't be afraid to reach out to a licensed psychotherapist to help you process the trauma. Trained professionals will always understand, even if no one else does.

Initially, it may be difficult to see the positive aspects of your experience. With time, you can process your negative emotions and see the benefits of your situation.

Setting Goals and Building Dreams: Chart Your Path to a Fulfilling Future

Have you thought about where you want to be in life a few years from now? This is vital because if you don't know where you want to go, how will you know what direction to follow? You can't and shouldn't live on autopilot just waiting for things to happen because of a bad experience. Otherwise, you'll get the same results every time.

Not reaching your life goals isn't as tragic as never setting new goals. The only way forward is to chart your path to a new, desired future. Setting goals and building dreams is how you do that.

Sure, it'll be hard to start thinking about what you desire from life, particularly because you've been conditioned to put others first and be selfless. A great way to figure out your true dreams is to picture yourself as a little one writing a wish list for Santa before Christmas arrives.

If you've been around kids consistently, you know they never think it could be impossible to have something they want. Why? Because they have no idea what things cost. You can achieve anything you dream of – if you don't think rationally. It makes you less hesitant about going for what you want.

Goals are key to happiness and success. Therefore, they should be written down. et a piece of paper and a pen to establish goals for the life you envision. Then, create two columns on the paper. In the first column, list 50 things you want to learn, do, own, achieve, or change. Write down a time limit next to each goal in the second column.

Now, grab another sheet of paper and list down the goals you aim to achieve within the next year. Leave a few lines between each dream. You can motivate yourself by visualizing the rewards of achieving those goals.

For stronger motivation, think about what you've achieved in the past that once seemed frightening, challenging, or impossible. Write down five of these accomplishments. Let them serve as reminders that you're capable of doing great things.

Visualize yourself at the bottom of a ladder. Your goal is to get on top. Don't think about the ladder's height or the number of rungs. Just think about what your very first step would be. Once you do that, climbing your way up will be easier.

Goal-Setting Exercise

This simple exercise is powerful enough to help you set goals and achieve your dreams.

Step 1: Dream Big

First, take a moment to think about what you want in life. What dreams have you always had? What makes you excited about the future? Write these dreams down, no matter how big or small they seem. Don't hold back. This is your chance to let your imagination run wild.

Step 2: Break It Down

Next, pick one dream from your list. Let's focus on making it a reality. Ask yourself, "What steps do I need to take to achieve this dream?" Write down each step, no matter how tiny. Breaking your dream into smaller tasks makes it more manageable and less overwhelming.

Step 3: Set SMART Goals

Now, let's turn those steps into SMART goals. Your goals should be Specific, Measurable, Achievable, Relevant, and Time-bound. For example, instead of saying, "I want to write a book," you could say, "I will write one chapter a month for the next twelve months."

Step 4: Create a Plan

With your SMART goals in hand, create a plan. What will you do each day, week, or month to move closer to your dream? Write down your plan and keep it somewhere you can see it often. This will keep you focused and motivated.

Step 5: Stay Flexible

Life can be unpredictable, and that's OK. If something doesn't go according to plan, don't be hard on yourself. Adjust your plan as needed, but keep your eyes on your dream. Flexibility is key to staying on track.

Take it one step at a time. Be kind to yourself, stay focused on your dreams, and don't give up. You have the power to create the future you want.

Embracing New Challenges: Step Outside Your Comfort Zone and Discovering Potential.

It's natural to want to recoil into a safe, familiar space within yourself after abuse. But that's now how growth works. You cannot grow in your comfort zone. Growth exists out there, in the unknown. That's where you can find out the extent of your capability. You've already taken an immensely courageous step by starting this healing process. Imagine what you could achieve by pushing yourself a little further.

There's an inner strength born from your experiences, even if you don't know it yet. Surviving the narcissistic dynamic increases your resilience and sense of awareness. Both qualities will be incredible tools as you face new challenges in life. Keep in mind that challenges are inevitable. So, trust these qualities, and trust in yourself.

Here's an important reminder: it's OK to fail. It's more than OK – it's a part of the process. Every failure or setback provides a learning opportunity. It gives you a chance to adapt and grow. So, do not let yourself be held back by the fear of failure.

The following are some of my favorite tips for stepping outside your comfort zone:

- **Attend a Meetup or Networking Event**: Go to local meetups or networking events near you. They can be nerve-wracking, but you will meet new people and expand your social circle. Plus, you get to learn something new, contributing to your growth.
- **Try a New Workout Class**: Remember what I said about physical activity as a way of nourishing your mind, body, and soul. Joining a workout class can help you push your physical boundaries and meet more new people. It's a win-win for your body and social life.
- **Take a Solo Trip**: If you've never considered taking solo trips, now is the time to start. Plan a day trip or weekend getaway on your own. Exploring a new place by yourself feels empowering. It can be a great way to build confidence and independence. You'll learn to rely on yourself and handle unexpected situations.
- **Volunteer for a Leadership Role**. Whether at work or a local group, volunteer to head a project or event. This is a great way to push yourself and hone confidence in your leadership skills.
- **Sign Up for a Public Speaking Course**. Public speaking is a common fear, but facing it head-on can be incredibly rewarding. Look for a public speaking course or join a group like Toastmasters. It's a structured way to improve your skills and meet others working on the same challenge.

- **Try an Unfamiliar Cuisine**. Go to a restaurant that serves food you've never tried before. It's a simple way to push your boundaries and experience new flavors. You might discover a new favorite dish!
- **Reach Out to Someone You Admire.** Reach out via email or message to someone you admire but haven't met yet. It could be a professional in your field, an author, or an artist. Express your admiration and ask a question. You might be surprised by the response!
- **Commit to a 30-Day Challenge**. Pick something that scares you and commit to doing it for 30 days. This could be anything from writing a daily journal to practicing a new language. The key is consistency and pushing yourself a little every day.
- **Attend a Workshop or Class Alone**. Sign up for a workshop or class on a topic that interests you, but go alone. It forces you to interact with new people and leave your social circle.
- **Speak Up in Work Meetings**. If you're usually quiet in meetings, make a point to share your ideas or ask questions. This will help you get comfortable with being heard and can lead to more active participation.

You don't have to step out of your comfort zone alone. It's better to do it with people who uplift and support you. Strong social support can make a difference in embracing new challenges and building resilience. Your loved ones can provide encouragement, perspective, and a safe space to share your experiences.

Be celebratory each time you do something to challenge yourself, no matter how seemingly trivial it is. Be proud of your courage and progress. Every win is proof of your strength and determination. Acknowledging your successes will increase motivation and keep you on track.

The beauty of embracing challenges is that it opens up a world of possibilities. You start to view yourself in a new light. It's not merely about venturing outside your comfort zone; it's about connecting with the real you and your true capabilities.

So, what's stopping you? Take that first step today. You have already overcome so much. You have the strength within you to achieve great things.

As we get closer to the end of this book, it's time to talk about how you can heal your emotional health through the physical. Let's explore how holistic healing practices can make a difference in this journey.

CHAPTER NINE:
Holistic Healing: Improving Your Physical And Emotional Health

As evident from the name, holistic healing focuses on the whole – mind, body, and spirit. It is a wellness approach that addresses not just the physical and mental but also the social, emotional, and spiritual aspects of well-being.

Whereas traditional healing methods focus on treating specific symptoms, holistic healing addresses the root of the health problems. The goal is to find balance and harmony in all aspects of health and well-being.

Suppose you're feeling stressed or burnt out. In that case, a holistic approach wouldn't just involve taking medication. Instead, you might be encouraged to try meditation, mindfulness, Yoga, and other relaxation techniques to find inner peace. It factors in the interconnectedness of your emotional health, physical health, and lifestyle choices.

This approach works because it acknowledges the complexity of human nature. Different variables influence health. For example, if you're suffering from chronic pain, holistic healing might explore whether diet and exercise can make a difference. It helps to see the big picture.

Pay attention to how you feel after walking outdoors in nature or doing a quick, deep breathing exercise. That's the power of holistic healing. It centers on natural therapies for trauma, such as massage, nutrition, and herbal medicine. And if you have symptoms that require traditional treatments, it encourages that too.

Why are we talking about holistic healing? You need to take charge of your health and well-being. Self-care will help substantially in your healing process. Making lifestyle changes that will bring lasting results is much better than opting for quick fixes. The best part is that you can personalize your approach to holistic healing. What works for one person might not work for another, so it's all about finding what suits you best.

If you're wondering what this means for you as a survivor of narcissistic abuse on the path to rebuilding a new life, let me show you.

As you've learned, the impact of narcissistic abuse is usually so far-reaching that it affects not just your mental health but physical and emotional well-being, too. It also impairs your social life and makes you dissociate from your body and soul.

Traditional techniques such as talk therapy, counseling, and support groups allow you to express your feelings and begin healing. Cognitive Behavioral Therapy is also great for reframing negative thoughts and developing healthy coping mechanisms.

But healing won't happen with talk alone. Art, music, and dance therapy are holistic approaches that can help you process and express difficult emotions. You will find them particularly helpful when words fail you.

Now, I told you earlier that trauma often manifests physically in the form of tension, fatigue, chronic pain, etc. Yoga, Qigong, and Tai Chi combine gentle movement with mindfulness to relieve tension and induce relaxation. Acupuncture and massage therapy also provide relief from stress and physical pain.

Other approaches to holistic healing include:

Nutrition

Nutrition plays a crucial role, too. A balanced diet packed with vitamins and minerals promotes overall health and can enhance mood and energy levels. Some holistic practitioners may recommend supplements or herbal remedies to help manage symptoms like anxiety and depression.

Mindfulness Meditation

Mindfulness and meditation are powerful tools in holistic healing. They encourage staying present and can reduce stress and anxiety. Practices such as guided imagery and deep breathing exercises can aid in restoring control and promoting calmness.

Spiritual Healing

Spiritual healing is another component. This doesn't necessarily mean religion; it's about finding practices that nurture the spirit. For some, this might be spending time in nature, practicing gratitude, or engaging in creative activities that bring joy and fulfillment.

In summary, holistic healing for abuse victims involves developing a comprehensive plan that addresses all facets of well-being. This approach helps restore balance and evokes a sense of peace and wholeness, which can lead to profound healing and growth.

Embrace this gentle, natural way to improve your overall well-being as you work on healing and recovery.

Now, how do you incorporate holistic approaches into your life?

Nourishing Your Body, Mind, and Soul: Fueling Recovery with Food, Sleep, and Exercise

When it comes to living a holistic life, nourishing your mind, body, and soul is beneficial. This means caring for yourself in all aspects, from what you eat to how you sleep. From a physical POV, nourishing your body means following a healthy, nutritional diet, exercising regularly, and getting adequate sleep. It's not about becoming a gym rat or following a strict diet. It's about being conscious of what you eat and how you move your body.

From a mental POV, nourishing your mind means caring for your mental health and well-being through meditation and mindfulness. You must try things that stimulate your mind, such as learning a new skill, doing something you like, or reading.

Finally, from a spiritual POV, nourishing your soul involves prioritizing your spiritual well-being by engaging in activities that promote calm and inner peace.

Let's look at how you can nourish your body, mind, and soul to fuel your recovery from narcissistic abuse.

Body

After what you've experienced, it's normal for your body to be depleted and in need of major TLC. It needs the right fuel for healing and recovery. The good news is that you can nurse it back to health with nutritional nourishment, sleep, exercise, etc.

Follow these steps:

1. **Eat balanced meals**

Maintaining a healthy and balanced diet is essential to physical, mental, and spiritual recovery. Believe me when I say eating well will make a remarkable difference. Include the following in your diet to make it balanced:

- **Proteins**: Think lean meats, fish, beans, and nuts. Protein helps repair tissues and build muscles.
- **Good Fats:** Avocados, olive oil, and nuts offer essential fatty acids that promote brain health.
- **Whole Grains**: Brown rice, quinoa, and oats give you sustained energy.
- **Fruits and vegetables**: Rich in vitamins, minerals, and antioxidants, they combat inflammation and promote overall health.

1. **Hydrate**

I cannot overstate the power of water. Staying hydrated at all times improves physical health and energy levels, which can enhance your mood. Aim to drink at least eight glasses of water daily – no less.

2. Sleep

When we sleep, the mind and body take that opportunity to repair themselves. Everyone should get at least eight hours of quality sleep nightly. Establishing a calming bedtime routine can improve your sleep quality. Turn your screens off once it's 60 minutes to bedtime, and keep your bedroom dark and cool.

3. Exercise

By exercise, I mean all forms of physical activity and movement, including Yoga. Exercise doesn't just boost physical health, though. It's also great for emotions and mood. Try exercise or moderate physical activity for at least 30 minutes daily. You can walk, jog, run, cycle, or dance – your choice! The key is finding what you enjoy, and it won't feel like a chore.

Mind

To nourish your mind, you must partake in activities and practices that improve cognitive function and ultimately enhance emotional well-being. Similar to how your body needs nutrition and physical activity for wellness, your mind needs its form of nourishment for optimal functioning.

Here are some ways to nourish your mind effectively:

1. Practice Mindfulness Meditation

Mindfulness entails anchoring oneself in the present moment to heighten awareness without judgment. It improves focus, increases emotional regulation, and relieves stress. Begin with a 10 to 15-minute meditation session daily and gradually work your way up. Focus on your breath, sensations, and surroundings during the mindfulness practice.

Apps like Headspace and Calm can guide you through mindfulness and meditation practices. In the final chapter, I will also share my favorite mindfulness and meditation exercises with you.

2. Engage in Continuous Learning

Learning stimulates and engages the brain, keeping it active. It could range from reading books to mastering a new language. It all depends on what you choose. Set aside time each day or week to learn something new. This could be reading a book chapter, watching educational videos, or practicing a new skill.

3. Practice Gratitude

Expressing gratitude is great for achieving a mindset shift from lack to abundance. It increases resilience, improves mood, and enhances mental health. Start a gratitude journal for writing down three things you're exceedingly grateful for each day. This can help cultivate a growth mindset.

Soul

When I say "nourishing your soul," I mean tending to the deeper, intangible parts of yourself needed for purpose, joy, and inner peace. I also mean engaging in practices and activities that connect you to yourself, others, and the world. These can include spiritual practices, creative pursuits, or spending time outdoors in nature.

After narcissistic abuse, your soul might feel drained and your spirit depleted. But if you nourish them, you will heal from within and rediscover your true self. Here are some ways to rejuvenate your soul:

1. Engage in Spiritual Practices

Depending on your perception of spirituality, this might mean following a religion, meditating, or connecting with a higher power within you. If you aren't religious, spend time each day in quiet introspection. Meditation works wonders for connecting with one's inner self and finding peace. But if you're religious, prayer can be an excellent way to seek guidance and solace.

2. Connect with Nature

Nature grounds us and reminds us of the beauty around us. Walk in a park, forest, or along the beach. Pay attention to the sights, sounds, and smells in your environment. That is spending time in nature. You can also connect with nature by tending to plants. It is therapeutic and fulfilling. Finally, try activities like hiking, bird watching, or simply sitting outside and enjoying the fresh air.

3. Practice Self-Care and Compassion

How would you treat a close friend in your situation? Let that inform how you treat yourself. Treat yourself with the kindness and care you deserve. Be gentle; recognize that healing takes time, and it's okay to have ups and downs. Take baths, read your favorite books, enjoy tea, or indulge in activities that make you feel pampered and loved.

Try these various activities and practices and see what resonates. It's okay to prioritize your well-being and invest in activities that nurture your body, mind, and soul. You deserve to feel whole and happy again.

Let's talk about mindfulness and meditation in the last chapter.

CHAPTER TEN:
The Power Of Mindfulness And Meditation:
Untethering From The Past

The impact of narcissistic abuse can keep you tethered to the past, but you mustn't let it. Through mindfulness and meditation, there's hope of healing and reclaiming your life. Contrary to what you might think now, mindfulness and meditation aren't just trendy practices. They are rooted in ancient practices and backed by modern science.

Studies indicate that consistent mindfulness and meditation practice can help a person stay focused in the present moment, overcome stress, and gain a deeper understanding of themselves. As a survivor, they can help you break the negative thinking loop and achieve emotional healing.

Here are some benefits:

- **Regulates emotions**: Practicing mindfulness daily increases awareness of your feelings, preventing you from being consumed by them. You can observe your thoughts and feelings internally, thus decreasing the possibility of being reactionary.
- **Decreases stress**: Mindfulness and meditation have been proven to lower stress levels. They do this by activating the body's relaxation response to counter the production of cortisol, adrenaline, and other stress hormones.
- **Increases self-awareness**: They let you connect deeper and better with yourself, increasing your awareness of your needs, desires, wants, and limits.

- **Boosts resilience**: Both practices can boost resilience, making it easier to stay strong in facing life's inevitable challenges.
- **Better focus**: Mindfulness can improve your focus and concentration on tasks. This can be particularly helpful in managing intrusive thoughts and anxiety.

Here are some simple mindfulness and meditation exercises that I have incorporated into my routine. Choose one to try daily. You'll need a designated area for meditation and mindfulness practices in your home. This space should be free from distractions and conducive to relaxation.

Deep Breathing Exercise

- Find a quiet spot where you won't be disturbed.
- Sit comfortably and close your eyes.
- Take a deep breath in through your nose, hold it for a few seconds, and then slowly exhale through your mouth.
- Focus on the sensation of your breath. Feel it fill your lungs and then release it.
- If your mind wanders, gently bring it back to your breathing.

Body Scan

- Stretch out in a comfortable position.
- Close your eyes and take a few deep breaths.
- Start at your toes and slowly move up to your head, paying attention to each body part.
- Notice any tension or discomfort. Breathe into those areas and try to release the tension with each exhale.

This exercise helps you become more aware of your body and the stress it holds.

Mindful Eating

- During your meals, take a moment to appreciate the food before you.

- Notice the colors, textures, and smells.
- Take small bites and take your time chewing and concentrate on the taste and texture in your mouth.

This practice helps you stay present and enjoy the simple pleasures in life.

Mindful Walking

- Go for a walk in a park or any quiet place.
- Pay attention to each step you take. Feel the ground under your feet.
- Notice the sounds around you – the birds, the wind, your footsteps.
- If your mind wanders, gently bring it back to the present moment and your surroundings.

Loving-Kindness Meditation

- Sit comfortably and close your eyes.
- Take a few deep breaths to center yourself.
- **Silently repeat these phrases**: "May I find happiness. May I enjoy good health. May I be safe. May I live with ease."
-
- After a few minutes, think of someone you care about and repeat the following phrases for them: "May you be happy, healthy, safe, and able to live with ease."
- Gradually extend these wishes to others, including those who have hurt you. This helps cultivate forgiveness and release anger.

Guided Meditation

Listen to a guided meditation specifically for trauma healing. These meditations often include calming instructions and affirmations to help you release negative emotions and build resilience. Many apps and online platforms offer free guided meditations tailored to various needs, including recovery from abuse.

Incorporating mindfulness and meditation into your routine regularly doesn't have to feel daunting. You can begin with short sessions, even dedicating five minutes daily, gradually increasing the duration as you become more comfortable. Also, try to practice at the same time each day. Consistency aids in establishing a routine and simplifies to stick with the practice.

Healing takes time, and so does building a new habit. Be gentle with yourself and acknowledge the little wins along the way.

CONCLUSION

Congratulations on making it to the end of "How to Get Rid of a Narcissist: 7 Proven Strategies to Identify, Confront, and Free Yourself from Narcissistic Influence and Reclaim Your Health and Emotional Well-being." You've gained valuable insights into narcissistic behavior. You now understand its impact on your life, and, most importantly, know the power you have to reclaim your freedom and well-being.

Breaking free from a narcissist is no small feat. It requires courage, resilience, and a steadfast commitment to your well-being. Throughout this book, we've explored the depths of narcissistic abuse, from the initial charm to the insidious tactics used to control and diminish you. Identifying these patterns is crucial for breaking free, and you've accomplished exactly that.

The strategies you've learned are not just tools for dealing with a narcissist; they are life skills that will serve you well in all aspects of your relationships and personal growth. Setting healthy boundaries, practicing self-compassion, and reclaiming your narrative is essential to a healthy, fulfilling life. They will help to protect you from future manipulation and cultivate meaningful, interdependent relationships.

Healing is a journey, not a destination. There will be fluctuations, moments of uncertainty, and occasions when the past attempts to reemerge. But with the knowledge and strategies you've gained, you have what it takes to face these challenges head-on. Embrace the process of healing with patience and kindness towards yourself.

As you progress, continue investing in your personal growth and well-being. Surround yourself with supportive people who uplift and empower you. Pursue your passions, set new goals, and allow yourself to dream big. Your future is bright and full of possibilities.

If there's one thing to take away from this book, you are not alone. Many have walked this path before you and have emerged stronger and more resilient. There are communities and resources ready to support you, and reaching out for help demonstrates strength, not weakness.

You have the power to build a life full of joy, peace, and authentic connections. The journey of breaking free from a narcissist and healing from their abuse is challenging, but it is also incredibly rewarding. Trust your strength, believe in your worth, and know you can reclaim your health and emotional well-being.

Thank you for allowing this book to be a part of your journey. Here's to your freedom, healing, and the bright future ahead. You've got this.

Printed in Great Britain
by Amazon